What Is College For?

The Public Purpose
of Higher Education

What Is College For?

The Public Purpose
of Higher Education

EDITED BY

Ellen Condliffe Lagemann

Harry Lewis

Teachers College
Columbia University
New York and London

Published by Teachers College Press, 1234 Amsterdam Avenue, New York, NY 10027

Library of Congress Cataloging-in-Publication Data

What is college for? : the public purpose of higher education / edited by Ellen
  Condliffe Lagemann.
    p. cm.
  Includes bibliographical references and index.
  ISBN 978-0-8077-5275-3 (pbk. : alk. paper)
  ISBN 978-0-8077-5276-0 (hardcover : alk. paper)
    1. Education, Higher–Aims and objectives–United States. 2. Education,
  Higher–Social aspects–United States. I. Lagemann, Ellen Condliffe, 1945–
  LA227.4.W46   2012
  378.73–dc23   2011026597

ISBN 978-0-8077-5275-3 (paper)
ISBN 978-0-8077-5276-0 (hardcover)

Printed on acid-free paper
Manufactured in the United States of America

19   18   17   16   15   14   13   12   8   7   6   5   4   3   2   1

Contents

Acknowledgments

The chapters in this book grew out of a seminar that met occasionally from February 2008 to June 2009. Our meetings were made possible by a generous grant from the John L. and Sue Ann Weinberg Foundation and we are especially grateful to Sue Ann Weinberg for her interest and support.

Ellen Condliffe Lagemann (Bard College), Andrew Delbanco (Columbia University), and Robert McClintock (Teachers College) were the original conveners of the seminar. We thank Andy and Robbie for the energy and ideas they brought to the seminar and for their interest and suggestions for this book. We also thank those of our colleagues in the seminar who did not contribute chapters. They are (with then-current affiliations): Gregory Anderson (Ford Foundation), Karen Arenson (*New York Times*), James Axtell (College of William and Mary), Thomas Bailey (Teachers College), Benjamin Barber (DEMOS), Thomas Bender (NYU), Alison Bernstein (Ford Foundation), Kevin Dougherty (Teachers College), Roger Geiger (Penn State), Neil Grabois (Heyman Center, NYU), Stanley Katz (Princeton), Anthony Kronman (Yale), Roger Lehecka (Columbia), Ann Marcus (NYU), Mary Marcy (Bard College at Simon's Rock), Mitchell Stevens (NYU), Stephen Joel Trachtenberg (George Washington), Sarah Turner (University of Virginia), David Weiman (Barnard), Steven Wheatley (American Council of Learned Societies), Pauline Yu (American Council of Learned Societies), and Harriet Zuckerman (Mellon Foundation). In a variety of ways, they all influenced the ideas in the chapters that follow.

Ellen Condliffe Lagemann
and Harry Lewis

Introduction

Ellen Condliffe Lagemann
Harry Lewis

What is college for? What roles do colleges and universities play in American education and American society? Preparing individuals for success in their chosen lives, of course. But should higher education serve a larger public interest? The chapters in this book address these questions. Each chapter is devoted to a different sector or component of higher education and all are joined by a focus on what higher education does well and poorly, and what it might do differently or better. The book grew out of our shared interest in higher education, and the certainty that institutions of higher education are vital to the current and future health of this and other nations. It is grounded in our belief that attention to questions of purpose is critical to any commitment to strengthen the colleges and universities that serve the people of this country and the world.

The public and private purposes of higher education have not been central to debates about higher education in recent years. Writing about colleges and universities is not in short supply. Almost every former college president writes a memoir, and studies abound of one or another aspect of the vast U.S. postsecondary system. Some works are quite technical, detailing problems of access and quality and, especially since the onset of the "Great Recession," calling attention to a wide range of financial problems. Some are concerned with the inordinate expense of college and the implications of cost for equal access. Others simply add another chapter to what one long-time higher education watcher has characterized as "long litanies of failure along with generalized prescriptions for making right what has gone horribly wrong."[1] But few assert, as we do here, that a lack of wide public consideration of matters of purpose is itself a problem—not only for the nation's roughly 4,500 colleges and universities, but also for U.S. society in general.[2]

There are several standard explanations for indifference to matters of purpose. Some people presume that the goals of higher education are well known and widely agreed upon and therefore are not in need of analysis or debate. According to this line of argument, the purposes of higher education are economic: Going to college boosts an individual's prospective earnings over a lifetime. For example, a September 2010 College Board survey indicates that college graduates earn on average 40% more than high school graduates.[3] Society also benefits from the research carried out at universities, which feeds innovation and supports economic growth. That is all true, but the narrow logic of higher education's quantifiable economic value for individuals and society at large has eclipsed discussion of other purposes and other benefits and responsibilities. It is time for a deeper and wider conversation that engages not only those directly involved in higher education, but all people interested in the future well-being of American education.

How and to what extent should colleges and institutions of higher education foster a more expansive sense of public responsibility among, for example, young people headed for careers in finance or real estate development? How, if at all, should institutions of higher learning be asked to foster in their students a more active engagement in politics? In what ways should institutions of higher education be asked to participate in public controversies—for example, those currently swirling around immigration policies? To what extent do colleges and universities have responsibilities to contribute to sustaining the arts in America? Why should public authorities from the federal to the local levels of government invest in higher education? Are productivity gains and other stimulants to economic growth all that taxpayers and elected representatives should ask and expect? What about honesty, ethical judgment, intellectual curiosity, aesthetic appreciation, and civic literacy?

In earlier eras, college presidents mobilized discussions of higher education while they were still in office and in a position to shape the future of their institutions. Few do so today. Each year, college and university presidents collectively give many thousands of speeches. Their rhetoric is polished, but their words tend to be ceremonial rather than searching, anodyne rather than provocative. They speak of excellence, human capital, and innovation. They promise great teaching, outstanding research, and service to the poor and needy—something for everyone, benefits for all. Modern presidents aim to leave the audience confident in the institution's leadership, not disturbed or confused about its place in society. Their public statements are bland so as not to offend any of an institution's multiple, varied constituencies, especially people who might make significant gifts. As managers of large and diffuse businesses, they may also fear that almost any consequential generalization will leave someone feeling left out. Most likely, too, presidential rhetoric reflects diminished public willingness to regard college presidents or other once revered figures as moral and intellectual leaders. Not being expected to discuss the public problems that confront us all, they shy away from the difficult and contentious. Whatever the causes, college presidents today have not stirred public involvement in questions about the ways in which colleges and universities have and have not served the general welfare. We seek to ask the questions that the presidents no longer raise.

Doing that is important because in the absence of public engagement in discussions of purpose, private purposes tend to trump public purposes. Unlike private interests, public priorities do not emerge spontaneously, but must be deliberately defined through discussion, reflection, and debate. The collective benefits of higher education will not be asserted unless the public can be engaged in defining them. A student's future returns on his or her personal investment of time and money will seem more critical than the public benefits to be derived from ensuring that all students become people of character as well as of competence. An institution's prowess in potentially lucrative lines of scientific research will seem more essential to its mission than its participation in the development of an aesthetically engaged and broadly humane society. Unless there is public discussion that can help support the balancing of public and private priorities, colleges and universities will dance only to the private ambitions that ensure continuing high levels of enrollment and high ratings in the various surveys of satisfaction that give institutions a boost in national rankings.

Public indifference to matters of purpose, and especially to questions of public purpose, threatens the excellence of American higher education and all that depends on higher education. Questions of purpose are always essential in mission-driven institutions. They help to ensure that an institution will be effective in pursuit of its particular ambitions as well as responsible and deliberate in its response to external pressures and opportunities.

We do not have a simple remedy for public indifference to matters of purpose. We believe it is deeply rooted in circumstances that are undermining public engagement in many aspects of American life. We see it as linked to increasing assertions of the primacy of all things private. Indeed, we would suggest that current disinclination to engage in reflection and debate about the multifaceted roles and responsibilities of American higher education may reflect a slow atrophy of faith in American society. Historically, national aspirations have often been advanced in discourse about higher education. New programs and policies opening higher education to more and more Americans have tracked American optimism about possibilities for realizing democratic dreams. There are few signs of such optimism today, as talk of higher education seems to become ever more narrowly caught up in worry about personal and national economic competitiveness. In response to all this, we have chosen to take up the problem of purpose in and through higher education somewhat indirectly, hoping that the chapters that follow will entice other people to join with us in asking for whom and for what higher education does and should exist.

We should make explicit several assumptions implicit in our interest in questions of purpose. First, we are advocates for higher education. All the contributors to this volume have spent their professional careers as scholars, teachers, and administrators. We cherish the values that have made American higher education great, including academic freedom, collegial governance, and diversity. We admire historic trends toward increasing democratization and recognition that excellence comes in many forms. We value the range and variety of institutional types that exist in the United States. In pointing to problems or shortcomings, we are doing so as "loving critics,"[4] people who find fault in order to strengthen institutions they cherish.

Second, this is an unabashedly normative book, full of prescriptive "oughts" and "shoulds." Though not devoid of statistics, it is informed by historical analysis, educated intuition, individual experience, and personal values. All of us deeply respect inferences drawn from carefully marshaled evidence, but the chapters in this book were written to speak frankly from convictions we hold as individual citizens. The matters about which we write are controversial—the importance of civic education and scientific analysis, the distinctive value of both 4-year liberal arts colleges and the larger enterprise enrolling "the other 75%" of college students, and the need for reoriented professional education and graduate study in the arts and sciences. They are much more controversial, we suspect, than current discussions might lead one to think. We speak in normative voices, then, in the hope that doing so will encourage debate.

The book opens with a chapter we wrote entitled "Renewing the Civic Mission of American Higher Education." We are respectively a historian of education and a computer scientist, and former colleagues at Harvard University. Coming from very different orientations, we found common ground in our concerns about higher education, especially its continuing commitment to common aims and ideals.

Even though we are deeply skeptical of historical accounts that confuse change with decline, we believe there has been a slow, steady erosion of civic concerns in American higher education. As a result of the decline of moral philosophy and of the professionalization of the professoriate, among other developments, civic education is no longer a priority at American colleges. It is now regarded as a matter for K–12 education, and it is often peripheral there as well. The erosion of civic education at the postsecondary level has been countered by a variety of reassertions of civic interest, and we sketch four: programs of general education at Columbia, Chicago, and Harvard; the student movement of the 1960s; the so-called culture wars of the 1980s; and the service learning that began in the middle 1980s. Drawing from these historic examples, we argue that plans for civic education must suit the circumstances of different institutions, though all must involve three elements:

intellect, morality, and action. In addition, we recommend that civic education be integrated into the major or core field of all undergraduate programs, be designed to promote long-term, global perspectives, and be reinforced by institutional policies and practices that incorporate civic values. We are, of course, aware of the obstacles to heeding our call for a restoration of civic purposes and turn in conclusion to the matter of incentives. Like all those that follow, we hope this initial chapter will help initiate discussion and debate.

In the next chapter, University of Virginia evolutionary biologist Douglas Taylor takes up the challenge of sustaining democratic processes in a society where, as he notes, "the fraction of the electorate that believes in flying saucers is as large as the fraction that accepts evolution." Pointing to the common belief that anti-intellectualism is the primary cause of this situation, Taylor argues that academics should spend less time blaming other groups, notably businesspeople and representatives of the mass media, for holding such attitudes and more time confronting them. This will require acknowledgment that all views are not equal about all things—there is scientific knowledge that validates the fact of evolution regardless of theological beliefs to the contrary. It will also require that, despite competitive marketing challenges, colleges and universities avow their intellectual priorities rather than the facilities and programs that, however appealing to potential applicants, may misrepresent their *raison d'être*. The bottom line for Taylor is that standing firm against anti-intellectualism is central to the public purpose of American higher education.

Having considered two intellectual commitments—to civics and to science—that we believe essential to higher education, the focus of the chapters turns to different types of institutions. The chapter by Bates College president Elaine Hansen argues that contrary to arguments concerning the irrelevance and even the possible withering away of this relatively small sector of the higher education enterprise, traditional liberal arts colleges provide models of undergraduate instruction that should shape our thinking about every other sector. For Hansen, liberal arts colleges help their students become "liberated consumers," living an enlightened life in a material world. To survive, she points out, all of us—both as individuals and as members of larger communities—must consume food, natural resources, and information. A liberal education enables one to do so in mindful, responsible ways. Traditional liberal arts college are especially well-suited to achieve this outcome, she claims, because all are designed to encourage five kinds of competence: They help students recognize and cope with complexity, difficulty, and time in making decisions; they teach habits that help focus rather than fragment attention; they privilege active making and doing rather than passivity; they emphasize sustaining friendships and human connections; and they encourage people to embrace contradictions. Traditional liberal arts colleges, as

Hansen sees them, are "misaligned" with dominant cultural values, which may challenge those involved in sustaining them, even though this "misalignment" surely accounts for their success in helping people learn both to participate in and stand against the grain of modern society.

Paul Attewell and David E. Lavin, fellow sociologists at the City University of New York, take a fundamentally different tack. They observe that selective colleges like the ones Hansen champions enroll only a small minority of the 17 million undergraduates attending college today (that number is expected to grow to 19 million by 2019, they report). Presenting rich data detailing how different the experience of most college students is from that of the relatively small number attending more "elite" institutions, Attewell and Lavin counter the most common criticisms of the non-selective institutions that serve 75% of the student body. For example, to the critics who claim that graduation rates are too low for such students, Attewell and Lavin counter that graduation rates would not be low if proper account were taken of the fact that most students require more time to obtain a degree than students enrolled in selective institutions, often for reasons beyond their control. Many students who are considered to be "at risk" when 6-year time to degree is taken as the measure actually move on postgraduate work. Because access to higher education is of such clear advantage to the "other 75%" and has not reduced returns to investment for students who attend selective institutions, Attewell and Lavin argue strongly against recent curricular, tuition, and tax policies that threaten the relatively open access that has been achieved in recent decades. The United States is at risk of abandoning as failures, due to statistical mischief, policies that have actually been successful.

After two chapters concerned with the importance of undergraduate education, philosopher William M. Sullivan turns our attention to professional education at both the undergraduate and graduate levels. Since most students are enrolled in professional or pre-professional courses of study, it is in relation to vocational questions that Sullivan believes higher education can have the greatest effect. It is here, he contends, that "the practical imagination" is shaped, and with it, our individual and collective sense of "what we can make of our lives, and the things we may hope for." However, for professional education to realize its potential, Sullivan contends that it must undergo fundamental reform. Taking aim at the emphasis on expertise over and above ethical behavior that has become all too common in many professions, Sullivan argues for a reintegration of knowledge, skill, and ethics. This could help foster a more "democratic professionalism" in which public service is regarded as an integral component of professional practice.

The final chapter is by Catharine R. Stimpson, who has served as graduate dean of arts and sciences at both NYU and Rutgers. From her perspective, the graduate school is the "nerve center" of research universities, uniting in its aims teaching, research, and the preparation of the next generation of scholars. Despite its vital importance to all parts of the universities, Stimpson believes graduate schools are not well understood. After a sketch of the evolution of the graduate school, intended to demystify its aims and operation, she turns to the consequences of growth and expansion and how the best aspects of graduate education can be preserved amidst myriad forces of change, including globalization as well as the very American penchant for "re-engineering, re-setting, re-booting, reseeding, and experimentation."

This final chapter is a sage reminder that we live at a time when financial, political, and social circumstances here and around the world must compel us to distinguish between what is essential about higher education, and therefore must be sustained, and what might be relinquished or reformed. The costs of higher education cannot continue to grow unchecked. Matters of cost, of course, bring us full circle back to questions of aims and goals, and most of all, to questions of purpose, public and private.

Across different chapters, questions of purpose arise over and over again as they do—even when unrecognized and un-discussed—in any and all conversations about higher education. As we have said, they are ever present in worries about the financing of higher education, from financial aid to endowment policies; but they are also inherent in debates about the substance of the curriculum, the meaning of academic freedom, and approaches to academic accountability. They are implicit, too, in consideration of the extra-curriculum, including everything from the robust American institution of intercollegiate sports to an array of clubs, publications, and issue-oriented organizations. Without a conception of the purposes of higher education, there can be no sensible assessment of historic decisions about who can and cannot go to college, such as the 1994 exclusion of incarcerated men and women from eligibility for Pell Grants, or the 2003 Supreme Court decisions countenancing the use of affirmative action in admission. Without considering the questions of "for whom and for what," it does not make sense to speak, as so many do, of "college for all."

Higher education matters a great deal to our collective wellbeing as citizens of the United States and the world. But if we do not know where we want higher education to take us, it makes no sense to complain that we are not getting there. By stimulating discussion and debate about what we want and expect our colleges and universities to do, this book is intended to put solid ground under judgments about whether these institutions are succeeding.

The book does not include a conclusion. Since our hope is to raise questions and promote conversation, a conclusion seemed out of place. Had we included one, it would have reiterated our belief that sustaining the vitality of the American higher education will depend on intelligent thinking and talking about matters of priority, aim, and direction. Because we also believe that the overall diversity of the American "system" of higher education is an important source of strength, any conclusion we might have written would also have noted that we would hope that each institution will design its own institution-appropriate process for raising questions of goal and mission. There will not be quick or easy consensus on matters of mission, within faculties or among institutions as varied as Reed College, Evergreen State University, Bennington College, and Bob Jones University, to name just a few. Our contention is simply that there must be discussion. Finally, in such a conclusion, we would have reiterated a simple claim. Higher education exists for the public good. The question to which we hope to have recalled all who believe in the importance of higher education is how to articulate and advance that good with more deliberate intent. We believe that question deserves our best care and most searching reflection.

NOTES

1. Robert Zemsky, *Making Reform Work: The Case for Transforming American Higher Education* (New Brunswick, NJ: Rutgers University Press, 2009), 22.

2. There are exceptions, of course. For example, Martha C. Nussbaum, *Not for Profit: Why Democracy Needs the Humanities* (Princeton, NJ: Princeton University Press, 2010), argues that a misguided conception of purpose is threatening American democracy in the United States and around the world.

3. Sandra Baum, Jennifer Ma, and Kathleen Payea, *Education Pays 2010* (New York: The College Board, 2010), http://trends.collegeboard.org/files/Education_Pays_2010.pdf

4. A term we attribute to the late John W. Gardner.

CHAPTER 1

Renewing the Civic Mission of American Higher Education

Ellen Condliffe Lagemann
Harry Lewis

THE SOCIAL PURPOSES OF HIGHER EDUCATION

"Education Pays," proclaims the Bureau of Labor Statistics.[1] Earning a bachelor's degree after high school, the bureau goes on to explain, increases earnings by 64% and nearly halves the rate of unemployment. Of course, other sources offer more modest estimates of returns. One compensation survey calculates the annual return on investment for a degree at a leading college to be 12.6% per year, or $1.6 million over a lifetime. And yet, in a society of divided opinion about the varied higher education landscape, the one thing on which everybody agrees is that college produces quantifiable benefits for individuals. As the 2010 commencement season began, *New York Times* higher education writer Jacques Steinberg observed, "The idea that four years of higher education will translate into a better job, higher earnings and a happier life . . . has been pounded into the heads of schoolchildren, parents and educators."[2]

In line with this common sense, the social benefit of higher education is commonly attributed to the collective effect of individual returns. That calculation reflects standard economic logic. College becomes an engine of social change when members of previously disadvantaged groups achieve greater educational access and then become more productive. As Barack Obama said in his 2010 State of the Union Address, "In the 21st century, the best anti-poverty program around is a world-class education."[3]

Yet higher education has vital public purposes beyond aggregated individual economic benefits. Colleges and universities should be forums for invention and social innovation that benefit *all* of us. They should be repositories of culture as well as sources for cultural creativity. And they must educate students, giving them not only the skills they need to be successful personally, but also the values, ideals, and civic virtues on which American democracy depends.

For a variety of reasons, the public purposes of higher education, especially those pertaining to civic education, have, at most institutions, fallen by the wayside. Some past rationales for civic education are less applicable today. The composition of the faculty has changed, as a result of different incentives in the hiring and promotion process. Presidents and other top administrators are expected to be winners in a competitive, consumer-driven higher education market rather than shepherds of character and ethical growth among their students. Demands on colleges and universities for specialized scholarly excellence and demographic expansion have displaced efforts that lack vocal stakeholders. A flourishing multiplicity of worthy but uncoordinated agendas has crowded out higher education's commitment to the common good.

THE WHAT AND WHY OF CIVIC EDUCATION

The ongoing erosion of civic concerns within American higher education is alarming and dangerous. We live in a democratic society facing serious challenges, domestic and international. Global political and economic instability, a communications revolution that has undermined old principles of information freedom and control, damage to the climate and threats of ecological collapse, peril in the supplies of food, energy, medicine, and water in many parts of a highly interconnected world, challenges to public education at all levels, and growing social and economic inequality at home and abroad all contribute to a cacophonous national and transnational discourse.

Many of the current sources of contention originate from stresses that have been part of American democracy from the beginning. Our Declaration of Independence promises the right to liberty and also to the pursuit of happiness. But what if my liberty infringes on your happiness—when, for example, I expose to the world information you would rather keep private? How much economic inequality is consistent with the nation's promise of human equality, and how much regulation of economic inequality is consistent with the nation's guarantees of individual rights? Do my fundamental rights include the freedom to degrade nature to the detriment of others' pursuit of their happiness?

Grappling with such questions requires powerful, multifaceted civic education. Civic education, at its best, begins with the acquisition of fundamental knowledge of the U.S. Constitution and American history. It encompasses an active interest in current events and persistent public problems, local, national, and global—and a disciplined capacity to analyze them. Because value judgments are essential aspects of civic competence, it encourages reflection on the meaning of fairness, social justice, freedom, and equality, conceived as both democratic ideals and lived commitments. Finally, civic education instills a willingness to take effective action regarding matters of public concern—not merely to understand them. Broadly conceived as a tripod that facilitates thought, judgment, and action concerning questions of public interest, civic education must be central to the educational efforts of many different institutions, including colleges and universities, in all their various programs, departments, and schools.

Institutions of higher education should help their students focus and elevate national conversations about enduring questions. Colleges and universities should act as wellsprings of republican virtue. Colleges are communities, and most colleges are communities that include young people. They are a natural place for citizens to learn values beyond their own personal welfare, to see themselves as part of a society of mutual rights and responsibilities. They should be settings in which engagement with questions concerning justice and goodness is essential to daily routines. All who are shareholders in these institutions—from boards of trustees and governments to the students themselves and their parents—should expect and demand that they will help cultivate an active, responsible, and informed citizenry.

The nuts and bolts of civic education are a staple of K–12 schooling. And so they should be. Despite that, many college students would have trouble passing the U.S. Naturalization Exam. One survey reports, for example, that a third of college graduates do not know that the Bill of Rights prohibits the establishment of a national religion, and about the same percentage believe that the president alone has the authority to declare war.[4] Teaching the basics of citizenship in college is a bit like teaching grammar: Everyone agrees that K–12 schools should do it, but colleges must do it as well. Civic education is too important to be left only to the first two stages of education.

Above and beyond ensuring that college graduates know the basics of American institutions, colleges and universities have a broad responsibility for the future of citizenship. They have become the central switching stations of life in the United States and other democratic societies. Free societies will not thrive unless colleges, graduate schools, and professional schools understand that the civic health of the nation is one of their central responsibilities.[5]

Sadly, however, civic education is too often marginalized at tertiary institutions. Expertise drives educational programming at the college level, and the specialization of the faculty has left citizenship as nobody's specialty. As a result, civics are easily belittled as an unworthy utilization of a research faculty, or shunned as a form of nationalistic indoctrination alien to the skeptical, freethinking academic world. The internationalization of both the student and faculty bodies has also made any hint of patriotic pride vulnerable to deconstruction as American-centric arrogance. Faculty autonomy, faculty allegiance to their disciplines, and the hands-off sanctity of the classroom at many institutions, especially the more elite, all further weigh against commitment to any common learning experience for all students or thematic coordination across the curriculum. No institution would explicitly oppose civic education, and yet many find it convenient to avoid.

In addition, in these times of deep ideological division, civic idealism risks politicization. The dual ideals of personal liberty and human equality have always evolved in tension with one another, but political advocates tend to stress one without acknowledging the importance of the other. In this way, calls for civic idealism in college can be stand-ins for both conservative and liberal political agendas. Worse, a call for the restoration of civic values to higher education that is balanced even slightly to the left or the right of center can be caricatured by the other side as proselytizing an extreme social agenda, either for socialism or for unfettered free markets. Colleges, worried about charges of political bias, and already filled with divisive social controversies to manage, have a pacific rationale for leaving civic education aside.

THE RESPONSIBILITIES OF HIGHER EDUCATION

Yet colleges and universities, whether corporately public or private, all exist to serve public purposes. Accordingly, they should be held accountable for preparing students to be competent citizens, domestically and globally. This responsibility need not detract from other educational goals. It may be different in kind from the objective of imparting knowledge and skills for further education and career enhancement. However, there is no zero-sum, competitive game here. Pursuit of one goal need not diminish efforts to realize another. Quite the reverse is the case. What is essential is for colleges and universities to acknowledge that they will not have fulfilled their public obligations simply by adding to the national stock of human capital, no matter how well they achieve that goal. They must recognize a direct responsibility for the civic learning of their students, spread across the entire curriculum. Only in that way can they meet their full responsibility to contribute to the well-being of our society.

Civic education has important academic dimensions, but it does not end at the walls of the classrooms. Of course, almost every college president lauds student "public service," but too often institutional support for it is limited to community service and volunteering. Rarely do universities encourage government service, either civil or military, or seek to engage students in local or state politics. Colleges and universities must help address our great national problems: the deficiencies of our health care and education systems, the degradation of our natural environment, the decline of our housing and physical infrastructure, the venality of our political system, the public consequences of our unstable financial system, and growing alienation from the very idea of government. In doing so, they will avow their responsibility to model at the institutional level the civic engagement they seek to nurture in their students.

To teach civic responsibilities, institutions must practice civic responsibility. They could, and should, do far more than they currently do.

OVERVIEW OF THIS CHAPTER

Before proposing remedies, we shall review how colleges and universities lost their sense of civic mission over the past century and a half, even as they have grown and prospered in almost every other way. Then we shall turn to the reactive forces over the past century—various movements and public debates that attempted to pull universities back to their civic roots.

Armed with an understanding of how higher education got where it is today, we then focus on the conditions needed to improve civic education in colleges and universities. As we have said, we believe that effective civic education must simultaneously involve students' capacities for thinking intellectually, for making moral judgments, and for taking actions that bridge ideas and norms. This is what we shall refer to as the tripod of civic education and we shall suggest this tripod as a framework for any effort to enliven civic learning. Colleges and universities too often view themselves as agencies of ideas alone, teaching students a version of the life of the mind or inducting them into a profession that is morally hollow or abstracted from the dilemmas of the "real world." As part of their mission to invent, preserve, disseminate, and apply knowledge, colleges and universities must commit themselves to discovering their own civic missions. Doing so is not peripheral, but rather essential to their educational effectiveness.

We offer, finally, three proposals to reanimate civic education. First is the heretical thought that general education and core requirements are *not* the right way to make the case to students for moral and civic responsibility. Schools, programs, departments, and majors are the centers of the academic enterprise. It is there that students must be engaged in civic learning. Second, given all the pressures for students to focus on short-term results, the single key goal of civic education should be to get students to focus on the big problems of the world, problems beyond single human lives or any individual's home community. The way to create a better world is for institutions of higher education to enlighten students to their own responsibilities and agency. Finally, we believe colleges and universities must become more self-conscious and deliberate in their modeling of civic virtue. They must teach and model that in all that they do.

We are aware that in both substance and style our argument is grounded in normative judgments for which we offer relatively little empirical support and none that is quantitative. We accept that our posture may be less persuasive in some quarters because it is ultimately grounded in morals. By candidly presenting our belief that ethics are inherent in all educational enterprises and are best and most honestly served when made explicit, we hope to provoke thinking and talk about what it is we want and expect from a sector of American society that is vital to all of us. Our goal is not necessarily consensus. It is consideration and conversation that we seek.

CIVIC COMMITMENTS IN THE HISTORY OF AMERICAN EDUCATION: A SLOW AND INADVERTENT DECLINE

From the Principles of Humanity to the Decline of Moral Philosophy

American schooling was never just about the three R's—readin', 'ritin', and 'rithmetic. The founders believed that civic and moral values were important to the survival of imperiled democracy, so important that "values education" was from the beginning a job for the state and not something to be left to parents alone. John Adams's words in the Massachusetts Constitution (1780) elegantly explain that school, and even higher education, were most certainly about personal development as well as useful skills:

> Wisdom, and knowledge, as well as virtue, diffused generally among the body of the people, being necessary for the preservation of their rights and liberties; and as these depend on spreading the opportunities and advantages of education in the various parts of the country, and among the different orders of the people, it shall be the duty of legislatures and magistrates, in all future periods of this commonwealth, to cherish the interests of literature and the sciences, and all seminaries of them; especially the university at Cambridge, public schools and grammar schools in the towns; to encourage private societies and public institutions, rewards and immunities, for the promotion of agriculture, arts, sciences, commerce, trades, manufactures, and a natural history of the country; to countenance and inculcate the principles of humanity and general benevolence, public and private charity, industry and frugality, honesty and punctuality in their dealings; sincerity, good humor, and all social affections, and generous sentiments among the people.[6]

In Massachusetts, at least, humanity, benevolence, charity, and even "good humor" are still on the books as central to the educational mission of all institutions.

The Roman republic was a model for the United States, and the founders drew on Roman historians and orators for inspiration. The grammar schools of the early American republic used Livy and Cicero as basic texts, teaching civic idealism and basic literacy in one fell swoop. Noah Webster, writing in 1790, trumpeted schools' obligation to instill civic-republican ideals:

> It is an object of vast magnitude that systems of education should be adopted and pursued which may not only diffuse a knowledge of the sciences but may implant in the minds of the American youth the principles of virtue and of liberty and inspire them with just and liberal ideas of government and with an inviolable attachment to their own country.[7]

Civic purposes echo through the founding documents of early American colleges, through Horace Mann's *Annual Reports,* and through countless Fourth of July and commencement addresses delivered to American students. Civic education was taken for granted as a basic purpose of education, not isolated as a separate subject. To be schooled entailed coming to embrace the common values of the American people. The *McGuffey Readers* and other texts that were widely used across the nation during the 19th century taught generations of Americans about the Constitution, American history, and the values associated with patriotism.

For those relatively few Americans who continued their education in college, civic learning was encompassed within the subject of moral philosophy, a capstone class, usually taught by the college president, and required of all graduating seniors. Debating clubs and literary societies used theses on civil government as opportunities for practice in public speaking and disputation.

The erosion of civic education began after the Civil War, with the ascendency of science in the academy and, after the 1870s, with the emergence of the research universities. Part of the problem, then as now, was allocation of limited teaching hours: as new subjects entered the curriculum, some older ones had to be downscaled or dropped. In addition, science was thought to be in fundamental tension with civics. Once conceived as a means for finding and understanding evidence of God's designs, science post Darwin became increasingly specialized and was stripped of religious and moral premises. Scientific developments fragmented college curricula and relegated moral philosophy to marginal status within departments of philosophy. As scientific knowledge developed along deeper but narrower lines of investigation, possibilities faded for instructing graduates in a unified approach to social problems and citizens' responsibilities to address those problems. As late as 1895, moral philosophy, taught by the college president, was still required of all seniors at Amherst College; by 1905, it was but a single offering in the Department of Philosophy.[8]

If civic education waned as moral philosophy became optional, two other related developments also contributed to its decline: the professionalization of the academic disciplines, and the emergence of the "imperial faculty," acting as relatively autonomous agents and only weakly allied to their institutions.[9]

Academic Professionalization

Professionalization in the academic disciplines was of a piece with the growth of advanced training and specialization in the late 19th and early 20th centuries. New institutions oriented toward research were established, and others evolved. Johns Hopkins University and the University of Chicago led the way for older colleges such as Harvard, Yale, Columbia, and Michigan. Increasingly, their faculty members were likely to hold a Ph.D. and to be engaged in scholarly research and publication. Most likely, too, they were members of a professional association, representing their particular field of academic pursuit.

Professionalization splintered once unified interest in social problems. For example, problems of poverty concerned different specialists differently. Sociologists might study the neighborhood origins of poverty, while economists and statisticians might investigate ways to measure it. In the process of subdivision, poverty ceased to be taught as a shared concern of all citizens.

As part of a further process of subdivision, social *science* came to be recognized as distinct from social *work*. Social science, being "scientific," pertained to scholarly study. In the ideal at least, its impartiality was assured through divorce from advocacy and social action. Social work, on the other hand, pertained to the administration and provision of social welfare services, and inevitably fell lower on the scale of academic respectability. As Charles William Eliot said on the occasion of his inauguration as Harvard president in 1869, "Truth and right are above utility in all realms of thought and action."[10] That pithy sentence explains a lot about today's academic pecking order. Traditionally female service professions—nursing, education, and social work—were less academically respected than the study of the underlying principles of the same areas—for example, medicine, psychology, and sociology.

By 1920, the University of Chicago included both a Department of Sociology and a School of Social Service Administration, which had grown out of the earlier Chicago School of Civics and Philanthropy. This movement toward academic professionalization and specialization is, of course, the way universities became great engines of discovery and invention. But with disciplines and professions parsed into ever more narrowly defined areas of expertise, separating science from service and theory from practice, institutions of higher learning became less committed to the advancement of broadly defined public goods, such as citizenship.

The Imperial Faculty

Faculty members were empowered by their expertise. Their allegiance and deference increasingly went to their professional peers, who taught the same subject to other students, rather than to their institutional colleagues, who taught other subjects to the same students. As their affiliations shifted from educational institutions to academic guilds, faculty members identified themselves more with national professional communities than with the local residential communities in which their institutions were located. With this cosmopolitanism came a related shift in professional identity: professors' disciplinary affiliations trumped their status as teachers. As this occurred, research, publication, and national reputation became more important to professors' advancement than their skill and devotion as educators.

At research universities, attention to teaching fell the farthest as research productivity became the dominant value. Provoked by dissatisfied students and families, and challenged by 4-year colleges, these institutions vocally reasserted their interest in pedagogy, establishing teaching institutes, institutionalizing small seminars, and generally devoting more attention to the undergraduate classroom experience. But good pedagogy is more technical and less holistic than good teaching. It pertains to the effective transmission of specialized knowledge more than to overall responsibility for students' moral and civic development. Ironically, therefore, the emergence, under pressure, of teaching centers reinforced narrow conceptions of the professoriate's responsibility for the overall development of students, which belonged to no one in particular, certainly not to any particular group within the faculty.

As national networks of academics developed across institutions of higher education, faculty members gained increasing power in relation to presidents and trustees. If they had sufficient professional prestige within their disciplines, faculty members could—and did—move from one institution to another if they were displeased with academic administrators. Donors, trustees, and college and university administrators, who once had wielded great power over their institutions, increasingly respected academic freedom and deferred to the wishes of the faculty. Increasing autonomy and power reinforced faculty tendencies to specialize and to devote their efforts to research rather than teaching and service. With no incentives for either professors or universities to cultivate humane values in students, civic commitments quietly faded into the din of the ongoing battles for scholarly excellence.

Science Triumphant

These trends, already evident before the two world wars, became more pronounced after 1945, when the report of Vannevar Bush, *Science, the Endless Frontier,* focused national attention on the importance of scientific research. Universities, rather than the national laboratories that existed in European countries, were identified as the most effective venues for scientific invention and discovery.[11] Federal funds for academic research increased rapidly. Today, every top institution of higher education benefits from federal research funds. Though technically awarded to institutions, funding for research rests on the knowledge, skills, and prestige of faculty investigators, who can take their research funding with them if they move between institutions. Dependence on research funds thus reinforced developing patterns of deference and power within colleges and universities, ushering in what would become a system of national "star" faculty and boosting the standing of institutions that secured the most research funding. By 1969, sociologists Christopher Jencks and David Riesman could write of "an academic revolution"—not the student unrest of the period, but the overwhelming power of the faculty to set institutional direction. Colleges, which had once been "pillars of the locally established church, political order, and social conventions," now existed in a hierarchically differentiated system of institutions that resembled a snake-like procession.[12]

Social and Scholarly Progress, Civic Regress

The ascendency of science had a second and independent effect on the teaching of civic and moral values in higher education. Science became the model for the ideal in academic scholarship—objective, unbiased, universal, lacking in moral direction, and usually detached from direct involvement in the world. Scholarship would be regarded with suspicion if a judgment of its quality were justified by its normative implications. The absence of (overtly stated) values became a signal of academic purity. Academic prizes and faculty appointments were awarded dispassionately, on the basis of academic quality. Awards were given for the recipients' acts of genius, regardless of their human qualities. The ideal for the social sciences followed suit—qualitative research became less fashionable as reproducible, quantifiable, opinion-free research results became the standard to which young scholars were held. In the humanities, where the best work speaks to the nature of the human spirit, the demand for fair, unbiased assessment criteria is yet an unfinished project.

At the same time, the expansion of graduate schools (including graduate professional schools) turned some of the old, prestigious, and selective institutions into top-heavy "university colleges," in which the undergraduate programs served *de facto* as prep schools for graduate and professional education.[13] With the exception of a few institutions that are able to sustain distinctive niches, all colleges and universities lined up, one behind the other, according to rank, with the most venerable of the university colleges leading the pack. Today's *US News* and other college league tables merely elaborate and quantify a pecking order that was commonly understood decades ago.

Throughout the second half of the 20th century, American higher education continued the trend begun after the Civil War toward specialized expertise and professionalized faculty. Of course, in spite of the dominance of the faculty, notable changes did occur in the power structure. Donors grew in importance, creating tensions with the power and prerogatives of faculty members.[14] In some instances, administrators were torn between the priorities of donors on the one hand, and the faculty on the other. In pursuit of the funds necessary for preeminence, too many colleges and universities failed to sustain the missions they continued rhetorically to embrace.

Higher Education as a National Priority

In pre-industrial America, colleges and universities were elite institutions. Their social role was relatively minor and geographically localized. Before the Civil War, denominationalism and local boosterism encouraged the founding of many small colleges across the expanding territory of the United States, each with a program that responded to the demands of the local population.

The first Morrill Act of 1862 provided an initial stimulus to practical curricula at colleges across the nation. The government offered land grants to colleges that would teach "agriculture and the mechanic arts" (not excluding "military tactics") in order "to promote the liberal and practical education of the industrial classes in the several pursuits and professions in life."[15] This expansion radically extended American higher education, enlarging its orbit to include farming and mining and industrial engineering. Parts of American higher education became unrecognizably strange to scholars visiting from Oxford and Cambridge. On a trip to the United States in 1914 to lecture on the foundations of mathematics, Bertrand Russell was astonished to find at the University of Wisconsin that "when any farmer's turnips go wrong, they send a professor to investigate the failure scientifically."[16]

In the 20th century, colleges and universities became major structural forces in American society. They develop and disseminate the knowledge that drives the economy. Through both their admissions process and their educational programs, they sort people into categories and match them to their adult jobs and social standing. Though most students attend college near home, some colleges are national magnets, and the force of their attraction permanently alters their local demography.

Both globalization and technological advances heightened the economic value of higher education's outputs, both a skilled population and the inventions and ideas that make them productive. The economic importance of higher education spurred student demand, and in order to make those economic benefits available to previously excluded populations, Congress greatly increased federal financial aid. All these forces aligned to drive both institutional and enrollment growth. There were 2,004 institutions of higher education in 1960, 3,152 in 1980, and 4,084 in 2000.[17] Student enrollment, only 2,101,962 in 1951, reached 4,145,065 in 1961, then 12,096,895 in 1980, and 15,312,289 by 2000.[18] Ever more explicit and narrow vocational aims became increasingly common. According to the U.S. Department of Education, just one-third of all bachelor's degrees awarded in 2007 were in liberal arts and sciences; all the humanities together made up less than 10% of undergraduate degrees. More than 21% were in business, 6.9% in education, and 6.7% in the health professions.[19] By 2010, the president of the United States was calling for every American to complete at least 1 year of "higher education or career training."[20]

Somewhat paradoxically, the explosion in numbers of institutions of higher education resulted in institutional homogenization, not differentiation. Some specialized institutions evolved—excellent undergraduate colleges focusing on business or nursing or library science, for example. But the overall force of competition among colleges and universities was to make them more expansive and therefore more similar. Most, and especially the large institutions in which most students study, have tended to follow the vocational and professional demands of their constituents. Eventually, other great national trends and events would dramatize what was lost in dividing higher education into so many useful, practical, but unconnected academic colonies.

REACTIONS AGAINST THE "ACADEMIC REVOLUTION"

Throughout the 20th century, civic ideals have been reasserted in a variety of ways. We shall focus on four examples: general education, the student movement of the 1960s, debates about the canon, and service learning. None of our examples played out in the same way at every institution they affected, and their strongest proponents might be surprised to find them cast as joined in any common purpose. But each of these developments was born of a sense that the fragmented system of higher education was failing to serve some larger civic need of American society. We believe they help illustrate the degree to which, still today, postsecondary education faces a similar failure of uniting purpose, and for some of the same reasons. Though none comprises a template we would recommend for adoption, all can prompt reflection on what might be done to enhance civic education today.

General Education

The three paradigmatic models for general education were developed at Columbia, Chicago, and Harvard. Though each responded to distinctive original circumstances, all were meant to advance civic values and to defend liberal learning in the face of demographic diversification and academic professionalization. From these three progenitors, general education took a variety of forms in the 20th century as colleges copied each other's models and refined their own in response to social changes throughout the century.

Columbia. General education began at Columbia in 1919, with the creation of a yearlong course intended to introduce students to "the insistent problems of the present."[21] Coupled with a course on "Peace Issues" (which replaced a course on "War Issues" that had been created in 1917), "Contemporary Civilization" was designed in part to bring academic dispassion to the wrenching experience of the Great War. In a larger sense, as Daniel Bell noted later in a report to the faculty, general education was also intended to safeguard undergraduate liberal education from pressures for earlier professional preparation.[22] Subsequently in the late 1930s, it was combined with a humanities sequence that had grown out of a "great books" general honors course, to form the Columbia core curriculum.

Faculty allegiance to liberal education combined with demographic changes in New York City early in the 20th century formed the backdrop for the Columbia program. The crucial step toward general education had been taken in 1916, when Columbia dropped Latin as an entrance requirement—making admission far easier for newly arrived European immigrants, many of them Jewish. The public schools most immigrants attended did not teach Latin, though it was still a staple of independent school curricula. The general education curriculum thus served both intellectual and social purposes. It enhanced the cultural capital of entering students, who no longer had a common precollege educational foundation while also addressing widespread anti-Semitism. Columbia College Dean Frederick P. Keppel noted that Jews had above average "intellectual curiosity," which meant their presence in "the classroom was distinctly desirable." He wanted course work that could ensure the "cosmopolitanism" taken for granted among Columbia's traditional applicants.[23]

By the mid-1940s, general education at Columbia had evolved into three 2-year courses in science, the social sciences, and the humanities, intended to introduce entering students "to a comprehensive view of what goes to the making of an intelligent citizen of the world."[24] It has continued to evolve to this day.

To the extent that Columbia's experiment in general education represented an effort to maintain older cultural standards amidst a changed demographic and social situation, it bears continued scrutiny. As it did 100 years ago, America is again experiencing significant immigration. Now as then, immigrants first segregate themselves, and over a few decades integrate, adopt English as their first language, and intermarry. And then, as now, none of this happened painlessly. Writing in the *Washington Post,* former Florida Governor Jeb Bush and Harvard professor Robert Putnam recently compared these two periods, noting one important difference.

> We native-born Americans are doing less than our great-grandparents did to welcome immigrants. . . . To improve their integration into our American community, we should . . . invest in public education, including civics education and higher education. During the first half of the 20th century, schools were critical to preparing children of immigrants for success and fostering a shared national identity.[25]

Helping immigrants gain a shared national identity is not a unifying public purpose across institutions of higher learning today. Very much in evidence at some community colleges, it is virtually absent at the more elite 4-year colleges. The Columbia experiment may demonstrate how shortsighted that is.

Chicago. At the University of Chicago, general education was embodied in a series of shifting plans for organizing the first 2 years of college work. Robert Maynard Hutchins became president in 1929, and used his office to decry the vocational trends in higher education and to promote the "great books." During the early years of his presidency a "new plan" required students to pass five examinations, in physical sciences, biological science, social science, humanities, and English literature, before moving into more specialized work for the last two undergraduate years. (The first four of these examination areas corresponded to the four divisions into which Hutchins structured the university's 72 departments.) Hutchins wished to prepare students for these examinations through required courses built exclusively around classical texts. The faculty dissented, insisting that the "great books" be supplemented by more contemporary writings, so Hutchins's dream of a purely classical curriculum never came to pass at Chicago.[26]

Deeply influenced by the humanist philosopher Mortimer Adler (who had participated in the general honors course that preceded the humanities core at Columbia), Hutchins saw general education as a means for introducing students to the "Great Conversations" of humanity.[27] Though the Chicago practice never fully matched the vision, Hutchins famously laid out his rationale in *The Higher Learning in America.* Only a few colleges, such as St. John's College in Annapolis, executed that program in virtually its pure form.

In Hutchins's view, "general education is education for everybody" and is of just as much value to those not intent on advanced study as to those who are. General education was to be integrated into institutions of higher education, making the whole university or college more than a federation of distinct schools and departments overseen by a common administration. It was part of a lifelong educational process, extending beyond what is taught or studied in school, intended to nurture the intellectual and practical virtues—essentially the capacity to think rationally and act morally. Leaving the more practical lessons of experience to life beyond academe, general education was, in Hutchins's view, intended "to draw out the elements of our common human nature." Taking direct aim at people who believed education should reflect the political, economic, social, and intellectual changes occurring in society, Hutchins insisted: "Education implies teaching. Teaching implies knowledge. Knowledge is truth. The truth is everywhere the same. Hence education should be everywhere the same."[28]

Hutchins's rationale for general education has always been controversial. It was pointedly at odds with the professional specialization of the University of Chicago faculty—and the faculties of many other colleges. Ph.D. programs train experts, not generalists, and faculties everywhere have to be constructed from the scholars produced by doctoral programs.

Even more fundamentally, the spirit of great books and great questions was basically at odds with the practicality and flexibility characteristic of American education. But its aspirations to universality and timelessness are worth contemplating still. Such intellectual idealism is never out of place. The job of higher education should be to lift the vision of its students toward the highest achievements of the life of the mind. Then again, the pragmatism of the American spirit cannot and should not simply be dismissed or ignored as inappropriate. Especially today with so many more upwardly mobile students attending college, general education has to provide a bridge between the life of the mind and the life of commerce and careers. No broadly attractive program can be credible without such linkages.

Harvard. General education at Harvard was organized along a tripartite plan similar to that at Columbia. It was meant to prepare students "for those common spheres which, as citizens and heirs of a joint culture, they will share with others."[29]

At Harvard, general education was born in the midst of World War II, during the presidency of James B. Conant. One of Conant's major ambitions was to advance "meritocracy" by admitting students from a wider range of schools and regions, and to make their attendance financially possible through a program of "National Scholarships." General education was intended to provide the newly diverse Harvard student body with common knowledge. In Conant's view, "a set of common beliefs is essential for the health and vigor of a free society . . . The future citizens we desire to educate should have strong loyalties and high civic courage. Such emotional attitudes are in part the product of a common knowledge and a common set of values."[30]

Once again, general education was meant to counter curricular fragmentation and vocational specialization. According to Harvard's report, *General Education in a Free Society* (commonly known as the Red Book), concentrations or majors had become little more than "a kind of higher vocational training." This was a result of modern life in a democracy, the Red Book maintained. Since "the moneyed class is less strong and almost all young people have to prepare themselves to make a living," the report argued, the aim of general education was to establish "the common view of life" no longer available through common subject matter or methods.[31] General education looked to the student's "life as a responsible human being and citizen" and to certain "traits of mind and ways of looking at man and the world" that transcended vocational and professional specialization. "The heart of the problem of a general education," Conant said when he launched the educational review in January 1943, "is the continuance of the liberal and humane tradition. Neither the mere acquisition of information nor the development of special skills and talents can give the broad basis of understanding which is essential if our civilization is to be preserved."[32]

Harvard's general education program was the product of a time when the country was engaged in a popular war, widely regarded as being fought for the preservation of civilization. The faculty felt they could help the future by educating a citizenry that would not allow such a global catastrophe ever to happen again. Today, though America has no shortage of wars, opinion is sharply divided about whether the country is, on balance, doing the world more good or ill by fighting them. Whether colleges and universities can help in reconstructing a shared sense of direction, a common faith in the integrity of our national priorities, and wide mutual respect among people of different backgrounds and perspectives remains to be seen. But the aims of general education at Harvard, as originally constituted, may underscore the vital importance of having institutions of higher education devote themselves at least in part to defining and debating of what a "common view of life" might consist today.

Before turning from a discussion of general education to the student movements of the 1960s, one last observation about Harvard seems warranted. As the spirit of the Red Book faded, its curriculum faded, too. Harvard has adopted two general education curricula since then, one in the late 1970s and one in 2005. Both share the structure of the original Harvard general education program: students must select from a set of courses specifically designed for nonspecialists, and their selections must touch a variety of disciplinary categories. But both curricula lack a unifying value system, beyond the value of being "generally," not narrowly, educated. They have both operated in practice as distribution systems. Professors have not been uninterested in teaching in these programs. But their interest has not been about coming together around shared educational goals. Rather, participation has ensured that their particular academic disciplines receive proportional representation in the distribution of the centrally controlled resources; for example, fundraising efforts, faculty lines, and teaching assistantships, which accompany their contributions to the program.

A compelling example of the failure of such a constrained-choice distributional curriculum to address the civic aims of general education can be seen in Harvard's newest general education curriculum, though the problem is common across many institutions built around curricular distribution systems. The single most popular course at Harvard, as at many campuses, is the introductory economics course. Though it does satisfy a general education requirement, many students enroll in it either as the first course in the economics major, or as what they hope will be useful pre-business preparation.

This is unfortunate. It has been known for some time that studying a standard introduction to rational-choice economics actually weakens those moral and civic virtues with which students arrive at college. In a 1993 paper, three Cornell economists studied the behavior of students before and after taking a standard economics course, which emphasized self-interest as the basis for rational choice. Their study demonstrated that undergraduates were less likely to make altruistic decisions, and also less likely to act honestly when confronted with moral dilemmas, after taking introductory economics.[33] A civic mission for general education cannot be taken seriously when the single most popular general education course tends to make students care less, not more, about the welfare of their fellow human beings.

The post-general education situation at Harvard underscores yet another point that must be contemplated if the civic mission of American higher education is to be renewed. Distribution requirements facilitate student choice. That pleases students and frees faculty members from justifying why some classes are deemed important just because, to put it plainly, some higher authority has decided they are "good for you." The popularity of distribution requirements as a replacement for general education is part and parcel of faculty disengagement from education as the primary coordinate of their academic roles.

The Student Movement

If the three paradigmatic examples of general education discussed above represented top-down efforts to institutionalize civic ideals in undergraduate education, the student movement of the late 1960s was in part a bottom-up effort to do much the same thing. Remembered mostly for its association with national movements—the civil rights movement and the anti-war movement and, a bit later, the women's movement—the student movement was at its core an expression of the alienation widely felt among young people toward injustice and commercialization in American society. The target was the university itself. Students' feelings about the university were complex. The conjunction of a military draft and student deferments made universities seem at once both sanctuaries and prisons. Students' frustration with both the politics of the war and their own uncertain futures put the publicly significant acts of a college or university under close moral scrutiny. The institution came to represent everything about American society that the students wanted to change. Thus the student movement, despite its radically anti-authoritarian agenda and tactics, sprang from a concern not dissimilar from that which had inspired the general education movement: a sense that colleges and universities were offering an education that was useful and practical, but also shallow and soulless.

"Welcome to lines, bureaucracy, and crowds," proclaimed the Berkeley student newspaper in 1965, at the time of the free speech movement. Addressing new students arriving on campus, the *Daily Californian* continued: "lesson number one is not to fold, spindle, or mutilate" your "IBM card."[34] The free speech movement had been triggered the year before when students defied university rules regulating political activity, leafleting, and fundraising. When one former student was arrested, a huge crowd immobilized for 32 hours the police cruiser in which he was to be transported, while many students climbed onto the hood to speak. Within a few months, Mario Savio, one of the movement's leaders, was able to rally over a thousand students to take part in a sit-in at the main administration building. The immediate action was brought to an end when the police arrested 773 students and supporters, but the events in Berkeley sparked student action at campuses across the country.

The Port Huron Statement, issued by the leaders of the Students for a Democratic Society (SDS) in 1962, presaged the roots of the rebellions that would occur later in the decade. "We are people of this generation, bred in at least modest comfort, housed now in universities, looking uncomfortably to the world we inherit," announced the statement's authors. They then went on to lament that their experience in universities had not brought "moral enlightenment." Instead, the SDS leaders claimed: "Our professors and administrators sacrifice controversy to public relations; their curriculums change more slowly than the living events of the world; their skills and silence are purchased by investors in the arms race; passion is called unscholarly. The questions we might want raised—what is really important? can we live in a different and better way? if we wanted to change society, how would we do it?—are not thought to be questions of a 'fruitful, empirical nature,' and thus are brushed aside."[35] Running to 45 pages, the Port Huron Statement concluded with a critique of the ways in which "the university is located in a permanent position of social influence" and must therefore be the launching pad to redirect political, social, and economic policies toward the emergence of a truly democratic society.

Owing to its anti-authoritarian rhetoric, and its visible successes in changing campus cultures, the student movement is generally associated with the political left. But another student movement also emerged during the 1960s: the conservative movement that founded Young Americans for Freedom (YAF) and issued "The Sharon Statement." That manifesto was formulated during a meeting at the home of William F. Buckley in Sharon, Connecticut, during the summer of 1960. Even though its authors were also "housed in universities," their call to arms said nothing about higher education, instead asserting principles compatible with the group's anticommunist and antistatist agenda. Only two pages long, the statement asserted the responsibility of "the youth of America to affirm certain eternal truths." These were centered in "the individual's use of his God-given free will," which required the government to limit itself to protecting individual liberty and ensuring internal order, national defense, and the administration of justice. In addition, the statement argued that "the market economy . . . is the single economic system compatible with the requirements of personal freedom and constitutional government" and insisted "that we will be free only so long as the national sovereignty of the United States is secure" against international Communism.[36]

After the Sharon meeting, the founders of YAF worked with determination and persistence, mostly at the grassroots level, to move the Republican Party to the right. They were defeated when Barry Goldwater lost the presidential election in 1964, but the movement's efforts ultimately bore fruit when Ronald Reagan won the presidency in 1980. With that victory the conservative branch of the student movement achieved the long-delayed, indirect effect of reviving the earlier movement for general education—this time in a less academic, wider and more cultural and political form.

Debating "The Canon"

Questions concerning whether there is a single canon that should form the core of college curricula, and if so, of what it should consist, led to the so-called culture wars that began in 1987. The immediate catalyst was publication of Allan Bloom's *The Closing of the American Mind: How Higher Education Has Failed Democracy and Impoverished the Souls of Today's Students.* As James Atlas noted in 1990, writing for the *New York Times,* "Bloom's eloquent polemic" was "clearly a phenomenon."[37] In a few short months, it had sold half a million copies, and it remained on the *New York Times* best-seller list for 31 weeks—an astonishing run for a book whose argument dealt with the works of Nietzsche and Heidegger and other philosophers who are not household names in the United States.

Bloom's book was unabashedly elitist. In beginning his argument, Bloom, who was a philosopher at the University of Chicago, confessed that his "sample" (the term was placed in quotation marks as a token of his disdain for social scientific investigations) consisted entirely of students from the 20 or 30 best universities—those who, in his view, "most need education."[38] Even among such talented young people, Bloom maintained, a culture dominated by pop music and Walt Disney had created a generation of self-absorbed, sex-crazed zombies. The erosion of the humanities, especially great books curricula, meant that the universities offered little in the way of correction. Dominated by postmodernists, feminists, and relativists, university teaching only reinforced the pervasive mindlessness of the young.

Though Bloom denied being a political conservative, the worst excesses of the student movement figured significantly in his narrative, including an armed takeover of a building at Cornell University while he was teaching there. So, whatever his own politics, it was natural that conservative commentators would reinforce and extend Bloom's charges. Writing in 1990 as chair of the National Endowment for the Humanities, Lynne Cheney described universities as "tyrannical machines" more intent on generating new knowledge than on teaching established knowledge to the young. The university's failings in this regard were especially dangerous, Cheney maintained, because they were the institutions from which future K–12 teachers came.[39] By the end of the decade the alarms were being trumpeted not just about the degradation, but the de-Americanization of American universities. In *Illiberal Education: The Politics of Race and Sex on Campus* (1998), Dinesh D'Souza warned of a "new worldview" taking over American colleges and universities. In place of academic standards, admission was based on demographic categories; core curricula had disappeared or been diluted with non-Western authors; and required seminars on tolerance and codes for proper speech had diminished academic freedom.

Charges from the right were answered on the left. At the time of its publication, *The Closing of the American Mind* received some scathing reviews. Philosopher Martha Nussbaum questioned whether Bloom deserved to be considered a philosopher at all. Another review described *Closing* as "a book decent people would be ashamed to have written."[40] A decade later, in *The Opening of the American Mind: Canons, Culture, and History*, Lawrence W. Levine insisted that critics like Bloom, Cheney, and D'Souza had become "parodies of the very thing they're criticizing: ideologues whose research is shallow and whose findings are deeply flawed."[41] Placing their arguments in historic context, with a survey that ran from the Yale Report of 1828 through Robert Maynard Hutchins's defense of a great books curriculum, Levine argued that college curricula had to evolve alongside the continuous evolution of human culture.

In *The Twilight of Common Dreams: Why America Is Wracked by Culture Wars* (1995), Todd Gitlin, then of NYU, also aimed to contextualize debates about identity and curricula. The recent culture wars were, he argued, "symbolic melodramas" and part of a long history of American "purification crusades."[42] Economic decline and globalization had renewed American demands for clear, certain, and familiar identities. This urge for the secure and familiar explained the appeals for a return to a canon built around "great books" and conservative social norms. But it distracted attention from another shared need: namely, the need to reestablish a common commitment to greater economic and racial equality and better lives for all Americans.

Unlike Gitlin and Levine, who entered the "culture wars" debate to answer conservative critics of higher education, in *Beyond the Culture Wars* Gerald Graff urged that real education could come only from teaching the conflicts themselves. Rather than trying to mask disagreements about what is beautiful, true, important, or silly, the disputes should be opened to students. "Acknowledging that culture is a debate rather than a monologue does not prevent us from energetically fighting for the truth of our own convictions," Graff explained. "On the contrary, when truth is disputed, we can seek it only by entering the debate."[43]

Graff later amplified his argument by calling for the demystification of "academic talk," to enable students to engage in meaningful discussion and debate of important public questions. Without that capacity for reasoned argument, he said, students would be prepared neither to understand the conflicts between different camps, nor even to analyze the quality of different arguments. At a time when "talk-back radio, Cable TV talk shows, the Internet, and the reliance of politicians on opinion-polling" have become ubiquitous, we need "not only an 'informed citizenry,' but a citizenry that is sophisticated enough in weighing arguments to spot logical contradictions and non-sequiturs, not to mention outright lies."[44]

Civic education, while grounded in history and foundational documents, is indeed less about the acquisition of a single "canon" or core or official interpretation than about skills and understanding. Educated citizens must be able to listen intently and empathetically to other people; to analyze rationally what is said, read, and observed; to present thoughts clearly and to debate their merits vigorously; to confront unsupported assertions head on, rather than to dismiss or ignore them, or to talk past them with equally unfounded assertions; and, when appropriate, to identify reasonable strategies to take necessary action. Reasoned argumentation inevitably forces all parties to clarify their first principles—every logical chain must be rooted in evidence and clear lines of logic. Like all kinds of basic literacy, civic literacy, including familiarity with American history and government, is primarily a job for pre-collegiate education. The goal of postsecondary civic education should be mobilizing that knowledge to identify problems and evaluate options for addressing them. The civil conversation of democracy is not a point-counterpoint confrontation of opposing sound bites in which the two sides merely voice the glib scripts of their political parties. Real civic dialogue requires both sides to acknowledge that what they are discussing *is* a problem and also that it has no easy solution.

Service Learning

In the mid-1980s, yet another, quite different movement took root on college campuses to promote civic engagement and a sense of shared public purpose. This was the "service learning" movement, which began and mostly still remains an extracurricular, non-academic, and yet centrally educational enterprise. A significant point of origin is the founding by the presidents of Brown, Georgetown, and Stanford of Campus Compact in 1985, an organization to help colleges support community service. Campus Compact now numbers more than a thousand member institutions. Other organizations—for example, City Year—offer full-time volunteer experiences to build both civic awareness and leadership skills in participants, who work to reduce school dropout rates or the physical decline of inner-city neighborhoods. With the availability of such structured and safe urban experiences, often welcomed by colleges (though not usually for academic credit), some graduating high school students aiming for 4-year colleges have been encouraged to take a community service "gap year" before starting college.

Such efforts as these can be valuable both for students and for the communities they serve. Participants may learn things no college class could teach, and colleges rightly construe their support as a contribution both to the education of their students and to the welfare of the communities in which they are situated. Nonetheless, such service programs have not reestablished civic education as a central, rather than a peripheral and "extra," benefit of a college education.[45] Their strongest participation is by students from families with the financial wherewithal to fund their children's non-remunerative work, and at 4-year liberal arts colleges, where students search for indicators of public-spirited self-sacrifice to put on their résumés. In the modern American college, spending thousands of dollars for the privilege of building shelters in the Third World has more cachet than earning minimum wage as a lifeguard in one's hometown. However popular, these programs may not be effective in inspiring civic responsibility. A 2009 study suggests that students who participate in Teach for America are less civic-minded after their service than they were before.[46] Even though Teach for America is intended to inspire a lifelong commitment to civic activism through 2 years of service in education, as Michael Winetrip of the *New York Times* has observed, in fact, it "has become an elite brand that will help build a résumé."[47]

One of the attractions of service learning is that it tends to be politically uncontroversial. No one could be against helping others and learning how the less fortunate live. But the actual impact of such experiences is rarely tested. Indeed, as Gerald Graff has asserted, higher education is beset with "incuriosity . . . about what students actually get out of college."[48]

A report by Elizabeth Hollander, former executive director of Campus Compact, found that among the 30 members of The Research Universities Civic Engagement Network (TRUCEN), all campuses claimed that preparing "students to improve the quality of life in our society" was part of their mission. Yet only one institution was actually engaged in a longitudinal study of the outcomes of their work in civic education.[49] She discovered that, in fact, "faculty buy-in" was the greatest obstacle to developing effective programs of service learning. One Harvard respondent even told her that "faculty think of service learning as anti-intellectual and/or vocational training."[50] Though doubtless true, the comment was ironic in the face of the fact that Harvard has institutionalized a permanent faculty committee to ensure the educational vector of student public service activities.

On most college campuses, there is no shortage of volunteering—one survey found some 73% of undergraduates were so engaged—but little integration of such experiences with the academic side of student life.[51] As a consequence, service learning may offer opportunities for community involvement, but scant opportunities to learn how public policy might address the needs that the volunteers are serving. Many campuses have identified ways for students to work in soup kitchens or homeless shelters, but few teach the same students how public policies could attack the underlying problems of hunger and homelessness.[52] Both students and colleges, with good reason, feel virtuous, and a few students turn their extracurricular experiences into lifetimes of social commitment. But the majority of these young citizens graduate without the deeper learning they could later use to improve society.

In addition, service learning has not realized its promise as a form of civic education because the term "service" suggests charity, offering assistance to people who are poorer or in greater need than one's self. However heartfelt such undertakings may be, they engage students not as peers of other citizens, but as members of a social division superior to that of the unfortunate and disenfranchised. By focusing attention on the nobility of self-sacrifice and away from the republican spirit of reciprocal civic needs and benefits, service learning may, in fact, teach students to accept poverty and inequality as permanent conditions, rather than to improve social structures through civic and political means. The Carnegie Foundation report *Educating Citizens* relates a compelling example:

> A student volunteering at a soup kitchen . . . very much enjoyed the experience and felt that it had made him a better person. Without thinking through the implications of his statement, he said, "I hope it is still around when my children are in college, so they can work here too."[53]

More generally, the goal of civic engagement as currently practiced on college campuses has more to do with fostering social entrepreneurship than with nurturing what may be called "social citizenship." Individualism is still held in high regard in American culture, and admonitions about the value of diversity and collegial respect for differences do not extend to communitarian lesson about American society as a whole. To be sure, the daily news is full of stories about young men and women who have established tutoring programs in New Orleans, college advising for inner-city Boston youth, or food cooperatives that bring organic vegetables to church soup kitchens in Berkeley. Alumni/ae magazines brim with stunning tales of individual social invention that convey admiration and thanks to generous alumni/ae who have supported the establishment of increasing numbers of programs to teach social entrepreneurship. While highlighting the outstanding achievements of the few, such programs do little to promote a sense of social citizenship among the many. Social service on college campuses has become one more thing in which talented and committed students can excel.

The term "social citizenship" commonly connotes entitlements people are owed by virtue of their status as citizens. Social citizenship in the form of old-age pensions, mandated vacations, health services, and child care is better established in Europe than in the United States, and taxes are correspondingly higher to pay for such entitlements. Yet the term properly denotes not the benefits themselves, but their precondition: a shared view of the reciprocal rights and duties that citizens owe one another. As part of their responsibilities for civic education, colleges should be expected to foster such a view of shared civic obligations. Sadly there is ample evidence that they are not now fulfilling that obligation.

In our recent history, there has been much outside of academe that has helped to undermine social citizenship. Efforts to secure civil rights for an increasing range and variety of groups (African Americans, women, people with disabilities, and people on welfare, among them) have created a significant backlash. In consequence, questions of rights are often portrayed as a zero- sum game: If you gain a right, I loose one. In the divisive score keeping, faith is diminished in the common rights and obligations of social citizenship.

In addition, political efforts to portray "the government" as distanced from "the people" have been stunningly successful, even among people who do not fully subscribe to the conservative ideology that made this division a staple of political rhetoric. To most of us, government represents faceless bureaucracies that intrude into our lives in annoying ways: through tax audits, mandatory jury service, or cumbersome requirements associated with unemployment or disability benefits. Ronald Reagan touched a perfect chord when he announced that the phrase "I'm from the government and I'm here to help" included "the nine most terrifying words in the English language." Our knowledge of government debates and decisions concerning policies and programs that affect our lives is so mediated by expert organizations, political lobbies, and the media that such matters often seem not to be any of our business.

Efforts to reach across this divide by polling constituents are misdirected since our system of governance intentionally avoids direct democracy by popular plebiscite. Yet the failure of the system to respond instantly to the now easily administered opinion polls only add to public cynicism.

Clearly, the declining currency of public goods as goals of the college experience is in significant measure a result of the current atomization of American life. We operate as if we were disconnected, partisan, privatized islands and we seem to accept that state of things. By promoting social entrepreneurship, without corresponding attention to civic learning, higher education has unwittingly played a role in contributing to the problem of civic incoherence.

A WAY FORWARD

What lessons for the future can we take away from our analysis of the past of civic education in colleges and universities?[54] We will not offer a syllabus, a program, or a prescription for success. One size will not fit all: institutions are too diverse in their histories, their missions, and in the characteristics of their student bodies and their faculties. Our hope is to encourage interest, concern, discussion, and debate.

Even though we advance no specific prescriptions, we do recommend a framework for any successful program of civic education. This involves the tripod of intellect, morality, and action mentioned earlier in defining civic education. We are convinced that any successful program must encompass all three. With that in mind, we describe three ways in which efforts to develop more successful civic education programs can proceed. Those are placing civic education at the core of students' academic experience, their degree programs or majors; decreasing student myopia, both spatial and temporal, so that they will see themselves as part of a larger, enduring world; and modeling civic responsibility throughout all departments and policies of a college or university. We close with some thoughts on the ultimate question for any normative educational essay such as this one. We have attempted to explain what we believe universities *should* do, and why. But with all the other pressures and demands on them, what are the real motivations for universities to take their civic responsibilities seriously? The issue ultimately comes down to having those who believe the civic mission of higher education is vital to find ways to mobilize their colleagues.

The Tripod: Intellect, Morality, Action

Intellect. Colleges and universities are defined by their commitment to study. However important extracurricular or residential experiences may be for some students, no form of learning will be taken seriously unless it has an academic dimension. It is not by chance that "credit" is awarded for academic activities, not for ones deemed extracurricular. So it is with the curriculum that we must begin.

To make a serious commitment to civic education, institutions of higher education cannot sequester civic learning in a specialized corner of the curriculum. There are many ways in which a demand to include civic education in the curriculum can be met, and to the extent that such a demand is one among many competing demands, creating a check box for civic education may at least establish that the institution is not ignoring the demand. However, for civic education to be embraced as a *primary* purpose of the college experience, civic lessons should be spread across the curriculum, not concentrated in one course area.

Most academic disciplines and professional or vocational fields of study offer opportunities for reflection on issues of current political or social importance. In some cases the opportunities are obvious. It is hard to imagine a course in sociology, for example, that does not raise questions about the nature of civil societies. At some point in their lives, all professors have to explain to the uninitiated why their work matters to the world. This may be challenging. For most professors, the academic respectability of their work rises, not falls, when it is severed from the world of values. In the ranking system of the modern academy, in which the quality metric is the opinion of their disciplinary or professional peers, few scholars want their work judged by its larger moral, social, or civic relevance. Nevertheless, a commitment to civic education requires that at least some attention be given to the relevance of any and all subject matter to public problems.

To engage faculty in civic education, the practical, applied, and even vocational dimensions of academic scholarship must become a respected part of ordinary teaching, regardless of program, discipline, or field. This happens naturally in programs with a career focus and must now also become the norm in colleges and universities centered in the liberal arts. For example, if a computer scientist pauses in a class on networking to start a discussion about the relevance of network design decisions to the possibility of anonymous electronic speech, that should be a curricular plus, to be balanced, of course, against the costs of not covering quite as much technical material about network protocols. If a historian calls attention to linkages between past and present, that should not be dismissed as an anachronistic focus on the present, but rather as providing yet another means to understand how and why the past is important. If a professor of business administration makes discussion of current financial news a regular feature of her introductory survey, that should be understood as no less vital than theoretical discussions of management practices and principles.

As these examples illustrate, effective civic education requires broad faculty buy-in. Professors must recognize that their educational responsibilities involve more than providing the best training and preparation in their particular fields of expertise. In tandem with the administration, the faculty must come together to accept some common goals for civic education, and must be incentivized and rewarded accordingly. This will involve a shift of campus culture at most institutions, a shift that will be possible only with a shift in the standards by which institutions judge their success. We return to these driving forces later.

Morality. Outside our houses of religious worship, the subject of morality causes discomfort on campus. The academic revolution drove the subject out of the portfolio of professors. Faculty simply do not consider good and evil to be their business, even for discussion, much less judgment. The moral development of individual students is regarded as a parental responsibility, if indeed it is acknowledged that there is anything left to develop by the age students enter college.

Of course, every college has standards of behavior for its students, both academic and behavioral. But as American society has become more litigious, as the value of a college degree and an unblemished transcript has increased, and as students' legal rights to privacy have expanded, student malfeasance has come to be regarded more as rule-breaking and less as ethical or moral transgressions. It has become risky for colleges to reprimand students for violations of a general principle in the absence of a corresponding specific, precisely articulated regulation. When students are called up for their transgressions, the discussion then tends to be about the details of acts, and whether they fit the text of the codes, rather than the principles underlying the entire educational community. Of necessity, deans, program directors, and counselors act more like lawyers and less like moral educators. The accused student may learn nothing from the experience, except how to fight a charge. Owing to confidentiality the student's peers likely learn nothing at all.

The effect may be a process that meets important (and legally mandated) standards of fairness, but an important opportunity for moral education has been lost. College students—whether 18 or 35—are not too old to learn to be better people, or to be freed from the various forms of self-centeredness, prejudice, greed, anger, and jealousy with which they may have been raised, or indeed infused by the process of gaining admission or the resources to go to college. In the interest of graduating fewer Bernie Madoffs and Rod Blagojeviches, colleges should find varied ways to talk about *why* their standards are what they are and what kind of people their graduates are expected to be and not save such discussion for presidential remarks at graduation. Of course, some institutions do exactly that, but the practice is too rare in secular universities and colleges. The diversity of ethnicities, regional origins, religions, and sexual orientations that colleges justly celebrate need not drive all discussion of shared values from the scene. Every college year brings its teachable moments. The lessons that must be articulated in times of crisis are far more credible if they are only reminders of principles that were discussed on less volatile occasions.

But matters of morality should not be thought of only in relation to matters of rules, regulations, and community-wide events. They should be central to the concerns taken up in college classrooms. As we have said, there are opportunities in almost every discipline and professional program to raise issues of civic importance and also to focus attention on matters of ethics and values. Consider, for example, the study of economics, which is so significant for policy decisions affecting social progress in America and in the world.

For several decades the field of economics has been following the path already discussed: more mathematical and more scientific, and hence more respectable. The humiliating failure of most economists to anticipate the 2008–2009 global economic collapse provides, perhaps, an opportunity to encourage students to experience other disciplinary perspectives on economic issues.

We are not economists and we would not venture to suggest how economics should be taught. But if the modal common experience of undergraduates in business-related programs—and many other students as well—is a course emphasizing self-interest as the fundamental basis for rational choice, colleges and universities must ask themselves how a counterbalancing civic message can be considered through the study of nonprofit management, global poverty, climate change, or the origins and future of life on earth, for example. There is no shortage of instructive problems whose history and solutions would balance the interest of students in achieving personal financial success.

Action. Civic learning is about the effect of human decisions on other humans and on society at large. We have noted the benefits and limitations of the service learning model, in which students participate as volunteers in community or other public service activities, with the aim both of addressing some public problem and learning about that problem from direct experience. The most serious limitation of this model is that it tends to exploit, and reinforce, the separation of student experience into separate curricular and extracurricular dominions. Students are left to integrate the two on their own—or worse, to conclude that their academic experience has nothing to contribute to their understanding of poverty, hunger, or homelessness.

What is needed instead is the routine exploitation of the outside world as a natural laboratory for concepts discussed in the classroom. Needless to say, care must be taken not to violate protocols concerning human subjects and other ethical issues arising from learning in the field. But the difficulties involved in taking learning outside of the classroom should not preclude far more imaginative experiments in integrating the academic and the "real" worlds. This is already well established in some fields, which require practice from the outset. Nursing and education are classic examples. But integration is also possible in other fields and disciplines, in history, political science, architecture, and economics, to name just a few. Even if the engagement takes place in a traditional classroom, real-world concerns can be brought to the fore in most class discussions. In engineering, for example, there are clear opportunities for students to grapple with open-ended problems of the world from domains such as transportation, manufacture, and food supply.

Finally, of course, the university itself is an agent in society, and its policies and decisions provide ready material for lessons about civic responsibility. We shall argue that a prime source of civic learning is understanding the importance of institutional behavior of colleges and universities themselves.

Three Recommendations

Even though, as we have said, we do not believe that there is "one best way" to revive the civic purposes of higher education, we do have three recommendations for ways to move forward.

Integrating Civic Education into the Major or Core Field. We believe that
all undergraduate students should be educated broadly. This is true for part-
time students in vocational programs no less than full-time students enrolled
at 4-year residential colleges. Narrow vocational training may lead to a first
job, but it will not serve one's lifelong interests, when everyone is now likely
to change jobs many times over a career.

But our topic here is narrower. Because we live in a democratic society,
civic education is important for all students, regardless of primary focus, and
it belongs everywhere in the curriculum. Still in the American higher education system of the early 21st century, the most important place for it to appear is in the major or the essential core course(s) of a vocational program.
Civic education must be central rather than peripheral.

Regardless of field, faculty members care most about the subjects in
which they were trained and are expert. That is true for professors of Ital-
ian literature, modern philosophy, nutrition, Greek art, or fashion design.
They may teach general education classes or participate in a survey about
the "foundations" of education, nursing, or some other field, but civic education must be infused into the seminars and courses most closely associated
with the personal interests and specializations of different faculty members.
Only in that way will civic learning take on the intellectual excitement and
affective significance that make such seminars and courses special, a faculty
member's signature class. Courses in a major or professional core are, moreover, the ones in which professors have the best chance of speaking from
experience about the relation of their work to the problems of the world. It
is where they are most likely to be able to model for their students their own
commitments to improve society. It is where they can speak with pride about
the public purpose of their field of learning.

At many colleges, departmental meetings are the place where a commitment to civic education must be forged, if it is to take firm root anywhere.
They are the place where successes and failures can be shared and where
respected senior professors can model for their junior colleagues that their
civic commitments earn the respect, not the derision, of their most important
colleagues. At institutions more oriented toward part-time adjunct faculty,
discussions of civic education must occur as faculty members are recruited
and hired and must be evaluated as an integral part of a course load.

Promoting Long-term, Global Thinking. Students today are focused on
next steps—the next semester and finding the tuition to cover it, the next test
or the next party, a first job. Such temporal myopia has often been a characteristic of students. What has changed is that our major social institutions
are behaving just as childishly. Facts about energy resources are distorted to
swing votes in next month's election. Corporate decisions about long-term

investments are made on the basis of the demands for good numbers in an upcoming quarterly shareholder report. Of all the major institutions in American society, colleges and universities have the best chance of instilling respect for longer-range thinking. If they do not do it, no one will.

If there is one civic lesson we would like students to take away from their undergraduate experience, it is this: *You are responsible not only for your own future, but also for the future of the world.* Not that we expect everyone to become president of the United States or a titan of industry. Rather, students must be encouraged to understand that every decision or action, however large or small, will have an impact on the air we all breathe, the way nations will co-exist, and the quality of life for many people, some known to you and some unknown, some seen to us and some unseen. It has become a cliché, but students must be encouraged to think globally, even when they act locally. They must be reminded that just as the flapping of butterfly wings on the West Coast of the United States has an impact on the movement of air on the East Coast, each action they take has consequences far beyond what they can see. Our collective actions can affect whether the world will be a better place, or worse, and enhancing awareness of that fact must be a primary purpose of civic education in higher education.

Students, especially the developmentally unfinished students of traditional college age, are likely to hear such messages with some embarrassment and cynicism. The culture of youth has always been about living in the moment and on the spot, and imagining that there will be an endless adult future for responsible behavior. The natural myopia of traditional-age college youth has been reinforced by the focus of many colleges on the health and happiness of students, often at the expense of expectations concerning responsible behavior. Equally important, the short-term economic and vocational rationales for college attendance held out to most students has made it difficult to think about one's education in terms that go beyond immediate self-interest. If higher education is to meet its civic obligations, all the forces supporting atomized, myopic thinking must be countered with encouragement to understand one's stake in matters such as drastic disparities in income and in consumption, within the U.S. and globally; the threat of global climate change and accompanying ecological collapse; and the prevalence of preventable disease and hunger.

The Internet may have flattened the world, as Thomas Friedman has told us, but Americans are less knowledgeable about international affairs than they were before the Internet came into being. Higher education must take that as a challenge. The percentage of TV newscasts devoted to international news has decreased from 35% in 1970 to just 12% today.[55] If colleges and universities do not cultivate civic knowledge and global perspectives, the airwaves will remain "the wasteland" Newton Minow warned about many years ago.[56] The prospects of ecological catastrophe are not new. As Jared Diamond has taught us, if we see ourselves as participants in a particular moment in a long human history, our natural resource problems seem much less improbable. Civilizations have collapsed before because of human folly.[57] Higher education must contribute to making sure that does not happen again.

To have students see themselves as part of a human story that is larger geographically and more enduring in time than the contingencies of their homework assignments and job prospects—we believe that should be both the goal of civic understanding and the inspiration that will make all of us take it seriously.

Modeling Civic Engagement Through the Institution. Institutions teach through their policies and practices, their governance and organization—through everything they do. No college or university will be successful in renewing its civic mission unless it is willing to scrutinize all aspects of its operations, from the meetings of its boards of trustees to its engagement with its local community and the wage structures for its department of buildings and grounds, to ensure that they embody the values articulated in the institution's mission. Civic education is not merely a matter of student instruction. It is not merely a matter for the faculty to take care of. It must be a concern for *all* those involved in leading and administering institutions of higher education. Civic responsibility is manifest in the behavior of governing boards and in the behavior they demand of those to whom they delegate responsibilities, presidents, vice presidents, provosts, and deans. Excessive compensation for those at the top has been much in the news in recent decades and is one of the most obvious ways in which boards have failed to align stated and revealed values. But there are others. Nothing is more damaging to the moral credibility of an institution than blatant lying by its leaders, and there are many softer misrepresentations that are, in the long run, equally damaging. These range from accepting gifts in "the public interest," even when the true interest is a pet project of some donor or the president, to turning a blind eye to neighborhood integrity and local land values when those may stand in the way of campus expansion.

As higher education has become an ever more expensive and competitive business, the ways in which decisions are reached have become ever less transparent. Public relations staff airbrush the underlying motivations for policies. Branding and marketing are essential in American higher education today, but some colleges and universities have press offices staffed with image czars who are incongruous in institutions devoted to discovering and transmitting knowledge. Renewing the civic mission of higher education will require that judgments about university policies and practices prioritize not short-term image management, but the deliberate and reasoned search for truth. Unless colleges and universities model open and enlightened decision-making, there can be little reason to hope that their alumni/ae will do so.

Institutions of higher education are agents in society and all their decisions provide ready material for lessons about civic responsibility. What are the admissions and recruitment policies and what purposes, institutional and public, does the institution think they serve? If there is an endowment, how is it invested? From whom does the institution acquire its goods and services? Perhaps most important, what are the priorities revealed through differences among departments and schools?

At many institutions, those departments and schools that are most directly aligned with public services—public health, education, and social work, notable among them—are much less generously supported than are those representing more highly remunerated professions—such as medicine, business, and law. Such discrepancies may be understandable in light of differentials in alumni/ae giving. Still, they reinforce the second-class status of the "caring" professions in which women have traditionally predominated. Recognizing that, some institutions have created loan forgiveness programs and scholarships for students in public service fields. Like service learning, those resonate of charity and do not address the systemic issues involved. Finding ways to elevate public service will be a prime challenge to institutions concerned with civic learning.

Where Are the Incentives?

Higher education has become a very complex, competitive business. We cannot say that a renewed emphasis on civic education is likely to yield a quick payoff. It probably will not raise an institution's ranking in *U.S. News & World Report*. It may not appeal to donors as much as a winning football team or a "leadership" program that carries one's name. We are also painfully aware that books about higher education are filled with exhortations, most of which, if they are read at all, are quickly disparaged and ignored as naïve and unrealistic.

Living as we do in a culture where policy matters are dominated by economic thinking, we have wondered whether there might be incentives we could recommend to foster movement toward a renewal of civic purposes. Could federal aid to higher education be tilted toward institutions that could demonstrate a robust commitment to civic learning? Could state and regional accrediting agencies mandate demonstrations of effective civic education as part of their reviews? In the end, however, policies mandating moral and civic commitments seem unwise. Any compliance they might bring would likely be superficial and technical. Persuasion, encompassing presidential leadership, collegial arm-twisting, and everything in between, is likely to be the most effective weapon.

Sometimes people are inspired to do good things just because they believe that doing good is right. Sometimes like-minded people can help one another do what needs to be done regardless of immediate personal gain. Evidence abounds that the world would be a better place with less greed and more altruism, less short-term profit taking, and more social investment. Perhaps the era of irrational exuberance that has led to so much environmental, political, and even personal suffering has come to an end. Perhaps dismay with political polarization and vast inequality will now rekindle the kind of civic idealism that has characterized the American experiment at its best. We believe the time has come, for the good of the nation and the world, to call our colleges and universities back to their civic mission. We can only hope that others will agree.

NOTES

1. Bureau of Labor Statistics, http://www.bls.gov/emp/ep_chart_001.htm

2. Jacques Steinberg, "Plan B: Skip College," *New York Times*, May 14, 2010, http://www.nytimes.com/2010/05/16/weekinreview/16steinberg.html

3. Remarks by Barack Obama in State of the Union Address, http://www.whitehouse.gov/the-press-office/remarks-president-state-union-address

4. Intercollegiate Studies Institute, "Our Fading Heritage," http://www.americancivicliteracy.org/2008/major_findings_finding3.html

5. We would include in our orbit of responsibility any institution whose students are eligible for governmental funds or which themselves qualify for governmental subsidies, direct or indirect (such as tax exemptions).

6. Mass. Const., art. V, http://www.mass.gov/legis/const.htm

7. Noah Webster, "On the Education of Youth in America" (1788), http://press-pubs.uchicago.edu/founders/documents/v1ch18s26.html

8. Douglas Sloan, "The Teaching of Ethics in the American Undergraduate Curriculum, 1876–1976," *Hastings Center Review 9* (December 1979): 23.

9. Morton Keller and Phyllis Keller, *Making Harvard Modern: The Rise of America's University* (New York: Oxford University Press, 2001), 215.

10. Charles William Eliot, *Educational Reform: Essays and Addresses* (New York: Century Co., 1898), 1.

11. Vannevar Bush, *Science, the Endless Frontier* (Washington, DC: GPO, 1945), http://www.nsf.gov/od/lpa/nsf50/vbush1945.htm

12. Christopher Jencks and David Riesman, *The Academic Revolution* (New York: Doubleday, 1968), 1.

13. Ibid., 24.

14. Richard Chait, "The 'Academic Revolution' Revisited," in *The Future of the City of Intellect: The Changing American University*, ed., Steven Brill (Stanford: Stanford University Press, 2002), 293–321.

15. Morrill Act of 1862 (Public Law 37-108, which established land grant colleges; Enrolled Acts and Resolutions of Congress, 1789–1996, Record Group 11, General Records of the United States Government, National Archives), http://www.ourdocuments.gov./doc.php?doc=33

16. Quoted by Bernard Bailyn in "Fixing the Turnips," *Harvard Magazine*, March/April 1991, 75.

17. *Digest of Educational Statistics*. Table 266: Degree-granting institutions by control and type of institution, Selected years, 1949–50 through 2008–09, http://nces.ed.gov/programs/digest/d09/tables/dt09_265.asp

18. Ibid., Table 189: Total fall enrollment in degree-granting institutions, by attendance status, sex of student, and control of institution, Selected years, 1947 through 2008, http://nces.ed.gov/programs/digest/d09/tables/dt09_189.asp?referrer=report

19. Ibid., Table 271, http://nces.ed.gov/programs/digest/d08/tables/dt08_271.asp

20. Barack Obama, Address to Joint Session of Congress, February 24, 2009, http://www.whitehouse.gov/the_press_office/Remarks-of-President-Barack-Obama-Address-to-Joint-Session-of-Congress/

21. Timothy P. Cross, *An Oasis of Order: The Core Curriculum at Columbia College* (New York: Columbia College, Office of the Dean, 1995), 6.

22. Daniel Bell, *The Reforming of General Education: The Columbia College Experience in Its National Setting* (New York: Columbia University Press, 1966), chap. 2.

23. Ibid., 21.

24. Ibid., 13.

25. Jeb Bush and Robert D. Putnam, "A Better Welcome for Our Nation's Immigrants," *Washington Post*, July 3, 2010.

26. Mary Ann Dzuback, *Robert M. Hutchins: Portrait of an Educator* (Chicago: University of Chicago Press, 1991), 127.

27. Gerald Graff, *Professing Literature: An Institutional History* (Chicago: University of Chicago Press, 1987), 163–167.

28. Robert Maynard Hutchins, *The Higher Learning in America* (New Haven: Yale University Press, 1936), 62, 66, 78, 85, and passim, chap. 3.

29. *General Education in a Free Society: Report of the Harvard Committee* (Cambridge: Harvard University Press, 1946), 4.

30. Quoted in Graff, *Professing Literature*, 167.

31. Ibid., 38.

32. James Bryant Conant, *Annual Report to the Board of Overseers, 1941–42*, Official Register of Harvard University, Vol. XLI, No. 23 (September 26, 1944), 13.

33. Robert H. Frank, Thomas Gilovich, and Dennis T. Regan, "Does Studying Economics Inhibit Cooperation?" *Journal of Economic Perspectives* 7 (Spring 1993): 159–171.

34. David Farber, *The Age of Great Dreams: America in the 1960s* (New York: Hill & Wang, 1994), 195.

35. *Port Huron Statement, 3,* http://www.h-net.org/~hst306/documents/huron.html

36. "The Sharon Statement," in John A. Andrews III, *The Other Side of the Sixties: Young Americans for Freedom and the Rise of Conservative Politics* (New Brunswick: Rutgers University Press, 1997), 221.

37. James Atlas, *Battle of the Books: The Curriculum Debate in America* (New York: Norton, 1990), 27.

38. Allan Bloom, *The Closing of the American Mind* (New York: Simon & Schuster, 1987), 22.

39. Lynne V. Cheney, "Tyrannical Machines: A Report on Educational Practices Gone Wrong and Our Best Hopes for Setting Them to Right" (Washington, DC: National Endowment for the Humanities, 1990).

40. David Rieff, as quoted by James Atlas, "Chicago's Grumpy Guru," *New York Times Magazine,* January 3, 1988, http://www.nytimes.com/1988/01/03/magazine/010388-atlas.html

41. Lawrence W. Levine, *The Opening of the American Mind: Canons, Culture, and History* (Boston: Beacon Press, 1996), 21.

42. Todd Gitlin, *The Twilight of Common Dreams: Why America Is Wracked by Culture Wars* (New York: Henry Holt, 1995), 2–3.

43. Gerald Graff, *Beyond the Culture Wars: How Teaching the Conflicts Can Revitalize American Education* (New York: Norton, 1992), 15.

44. "Clueless in Academe: An Interview with Gerald Graff," 2–3. http://www.themorningnews.org/archives/personalities/clueless

45. Elizabeth Hollander, "Civic Education of Undergraduates in United States Research Universities: Findings from a survey of the members of The Research Universities Civic Engagement Network (TRUCEN)." Jonathan M. Tisch College of Citizenship and Public Service, Tufts University, Fall 2009, http://www.compact.org/wp-content/uploads/2009/12/CivicEducationInResearchUniversities.pdf

46. Amanda M. Fairbanks, "Gauging the Dedication of Teacher Corps Grads," *New York Times,* January 3, 2010, http://www.nytimes.com/2010/01/04/education/04teach.html

47. Michael Winerip, "A Chosen Few Are Teaching for America," *New York Times,* July 11, 2010, http://www.nytimes.com/2010/07/12/education/12winerip.html

48. "Clueless in Academe: An Interview with Gerald Graff."

49. Hollander, "Civic Education," 12.

50. Ibid., 19.

51. Panetta Institute survey, cited in Anne Colby, Thomas Ehrlish, Elizabeth Beaumont, and Jason Stephens, *Educating Citizens: Preparing America's Undergraduates for Lives of Moral and Civic Responsibility* (San Francisco: Jossey-Bass, 2003), 8.

52. Ibid., 9.

53. Colby et al., *Educating Citizens*, 71.

54. The Carnegie Foundation study, *Educating Citizens*, cited above, offers case studies that are particularly useful for those seeking practical advice about civic education programs. They represent a very diverse set of institutions and also a significant range of institutional goals.

55. "International news as a percentage of American TV newscast." From Ethan Zuckerman, A Wider World Wide Web, slide 17. TED Global, July 14, 2010, http://www.slideshare.net/ethanz/a-wider-world-a-wider-web

56. Newton N. Minow, "Television and the Public Interest" (speech, National Association of Broadcasters, Washington, DC, May 9, 1961), http://www.american rhetoric.com/speeches/newtonminow.htm

57. Jared Diamond, *Guns, Germs, and Steel: The Fate of Human Societies* (New York: Norton, 2005).

CHAPTER 2

Science, Enlightenment, and Intellectual Tensions in Higher Education

Douglas Taylor

Faculty at colleges and universities are often characterized as inhabitants of the "ivory tower," a pejorative term signifying an exclusive focus on lofty intellectual pursuits too often disconnected from the practical concerns of the real world. Administrators of these ivory towers are charged with navigating the opportunities and tensions between the academic community and the rest of society. They grapple with the reality that the higher education system is funded by wealth generated in the private sector, and attempt to fulfill the expectation that the intellectuals should make discoveries that promote economic advancement and provide education that provides social mobility for its citizens. At the same time, administrators must insulate the academy from anti-intellectual and market forces that threaten the mission of higher education. How do you strike the balance between protecting unfettered intellectual pursuits of the faculty and obtaining resources from corporate or private philanthropy that has a stake in that research? How do you protect faculty from anti-intellectual forces (such as politics, the media) without further isolating the ivory tower?

An important first step is to recognize the tensions that exist, and identify their origins. Anti-intellectual pressures have a surprisingly powerful effect on college and university faculty. Many of these forces are generated by the usual suspects—politicians, the media, religious fundamentalism, corporate and philanthropic agendas. Other pressures are generated within the academy, or reflect the failure of the higher education establishment to understand and navigate them. Here, I relate my experience of being buffeted by anti-intellectual forces from inside and outside the academy, and how some degree of comfort can be obtained by defining one's own role as an educator in society and defending the importance of that role with confidence.

FACTS MATTER

My research is in a field, evolutionary biology, that is often poorly understood and the subject of unnecessary public controversy. The course that I teach, Ecology and Evolution, is one of three courses required of all biology majors at the University of Virginia. These courses cover the things we feel every graduating biologist should know, and many aspects of evolutionary biology naturally fall into this category. It is a large enrollment course, in excess of 330 students who come from a variety of social, economic, and religious backgrounds. When teaching a class on how new species are formed, we discussed vicariance. "Vicariance" refers to situations where physical barriers, such as mountain ranges, arise to isolate populations that were once interbreeding. Once populations are reproductively isolated in this way, they can readily diverge to form new species.

Vicariance has occurred in snapping shrimp in the Pacific Ocean and the Caribbean Sea, on either side of the Isthmus of Panama.[1] Approximately 3 million years ago, the Isthmus of Panama rose out of the sea and permanently isolated marine animals—including these shrimp—in the Caribbean Sea from those in the Pacific Ocean. The numerous species of snapping shrimp are therefore a beautifully replicated natural experiment that can be used to investigate what happens when such isolation occurs.

Nancy Knowlton of the Scripps Oceanographic, and others, found that many shrimp species coexist in the Caribbean Sea, but for each species, its most closely related population was in the Pacific Ocean, many thousands of miles away if traveling by water. In many instances the closely related Caribbean and Pacific forms could no longer mate, and were by any definition new species. This history was reconstructed using DNA sequence data to show the repeated independent divergence of Pacific and Caribbean forms, with dates calibrated using a molecular clock. The speciation events were simultaneous, geologically speaking, with the formation of the land bridge between North and South America.

This is one of the most elegant examples of evolution in action, where the findings of geology, genetics, behavior, morphology, and biogeography combine to weave a seamless narrative of species formation, in a replicated fashion. It is only with this historical narrative in place, with changing land forms and the generation of new species, that we can explain wide-ranging phenomena such as the apparently paradoxical distribution of pairs of closely related species that are separated by thousands of miles of coastline, while more distantly related species coexist as neighbors.

After presenting the snapping shrimp data to the class, I remarked that in all honesty, I found it difficult to understand how given such clear narrative evidence, anyone could doubt the existence of the evolutionary process. "Of course," I reassured the students, "I am not insulting those among you who don't believe in evolution." But then I paused and said, "Wait, what am I saying, yes I am!"

As the chair of biology at the University of Virginia, with an active research program in evolutionary genetics, I should be as prepared as anyone to project, with confidence and unapologetically, the fact that evolution occurs. In the 21st century, and especially in a biology class at an institution of higher learning, it should be as intellectually unacceptable to deny the fact of evolution as it would be to deny that the earth revolves around the sun, or that HIV causes AIDS. Up to that moment, I was unintentionally communicating to the class that there were two sides to the issue and that it is OK to deny evolution. In an enlightened society, that is not OK.

What are the pressures that make a tenured professor reluctant to assert that evolution is fact in a biology class at a leading university? First, faculty members recognize that many students are not academically prepared, especially in the sciences. Second, many are distrustful of science, especially when established scientific facts run counter to long-held beliefs. Thus, strongly held views about science can become driven by social, economic, or religious agendas that are not constrained by facts. This is a serious issue that the higher education system must actively work to counter.

THE IMPERATIVE OF SCIENTIFIC ENLIGHTENMENT

There is increasing concern that the American educational system is lagging in mathematics and science. This view is bolstered by the steady stream of statistics demonstrating that U.S. students rank well below other developed nations in science and mathematical literacy. Almost 30% of America's adults do not know that the earth revolves around the sun; over half do not know that electrons are smaller than atoms; only half the population is aware that dinosaurs and humans never coexisted; 15% of America's adults do not believe that humans have gone to the moon[2]; and one half of the U.S. population believes the human species was created less than 10,000 years ago.[3]

The consequences of educational inadequacies, especially in the sciences, are increasingly dire. Detailed reports from the National Academies of Sciences are quite clear about the high public return on our investments in science and technology, and the objective benefits that advances in science have for public health and quality of life.[4] These reports, however, are equally clear about a U.S.-wide deficit of scientific literacy. Scientific and technical knowledge is increasingly important in modern economies, and the ability of a society to produce, select, adapt, and commercialize scientific discoveries is critical for a sustained, much less an improved quality of life. However, it is difficult to imagine how a democratic process can make sensible decisions about, say, stem cells, if the fraction of the electorate that believes in flying saucers is as large as the fraction that accepts evolution.

The situation is more immediately dangerous when scientific ignorance, or worse, an actively pseudo-scientific stance is held by people in positions of power. Former U.S. president George W. Bush held the position that intelligent design should be taught in science classes because the "jury is still out" on evolution. Former South African president Thabo Mbeki infamously embraced AIDS-denialist claims. These views by leaders of very different nations are similar in the way they fly in the face of undisputable scientific findings. The former contributed to undermining science education in the United States, while the latter is estimated to be directly responsible for hundreds of thousands of deaths.[5]

A common theme in these discussions is that our questions about science are simply the latest incarnation of a long history of anti-intellectualism in America.[6] Anti-intellectualism is a distrust or hostility toward intellectual pursuits, and is often manifested as dismissing the importance of science, education, or the arts, especially aspects that are not immediately and tangibly connected to economic advancement. The intellectual is often dismissed as being elite, ignorant of and disconnected from practical realities. The intellectual's knowledge and appreciation of complexity and nuance are often seen as immobilizing, leading to a lack of decisiveness or conviction. The contrasting traits, which the intellectual presumably lacks, are an old-fashioned common sense, and a reliable moral compass of the right or wrong course of action which factual information would obscure rather than illuminate.

Anti-intellectualism, at least as described by intellectuals who write books on the subject, is often depicted as a vague inexorable force, with its historical center of gravity in the United States. It was Richard Hofstadter's classic thesis that anti-intellectualism is uniquely woven into the fabric of the United States, and that our history is one of cycles in which folksy populism tinged with an interest in business are interspersed with periods of economic collapse or feelings of technological inadequacy (e.g., in the wake of the Soviet launch of Sputnik) during which the academic achievements and the advance of knowledge, *per se*, are valued as practical necessities. Academics write as if these are two opposing cosmic forces, locked in mortal combat. On the one hand we have the major causes of anti-intellectualism, politicians, the media, religious fundamentalists, and even video games that converge in their opposition to critical reasoning and in favor of viewing the world in misleadingly simplistic terms.[7] On the other hand is the educational system, which is supposed to equip the citizenry with an enlightened educational background and the critical thinking skills necessary to make decisions that are in the long-term best interest of society and themselves. A rise in anti-intellectualism, therefore, is generally assumed to be a failure of the educational system to generate a citizenry that is enlightened enough combat these attitudes.

In most of these discussions, the responsibility for the perceived lack of intellectualism, or even literacy, is placed squarely on the failures of the American system of K–12 education. The National Academies of the Sciences have been consistent in their emphasis that the educational system is faltering, especially in science and mathematics. A most telling statistic is that in 2003 science testing, U.S. 4th graders rank near the 80th percentile among participating nations, but by the 12th grade, U.S. students drop to the 5th percentile.[8] It seems that the longer students stay in the educational system, the worse they do.[9] In fact, when the national academies were charged by Congress to identify nationwide steps that would help the United States remain competitive in science and technology, their recommendations relied almost exclusively on bolstering K–12 education, primarily by providing qualified, motivated teachers in science and mathematics and by increasing parental interest and involvement in our public schools.[10]

When it comes to sources of anti-intellectualism, however, the U.S. system of higher education is generally given a free ride. There are two reasons universities escape blame. First, institutions of higher education are considered the bastions of American intellectualism. Second, the American system of higher education is still widely regarded as the best in the world, and hence beyond reproach.[11] In the remainder of this chapter, I will argue that the U.S. higher education system must shoulder some of the responsibility for the current climate of anti-intellectualism, and should be playing a more active role in reversing it. I outline some general anti-intellectual tendencies in higher education, including the ones that are most damaging to society. Finally, I offer some suggestions regarding how to reverse course.

THE PLIGHT OF THE INTELLECTUAL

My class on the evolution of the snapping shrimp crystallized the fact that there were social and professional pressures to avoid confrontation on the issue of evolution. Evolutionary biologists face a multitude of anti-intellectual pressures. Our science is no less substantiated by scientific observation than any other science, but it has the unfortunate quality of being precisely what people, particularly religious people, do not want to believe. This generates conflict, and since religion is a personal matter, the instinct is for scientists to be civil. This is the generous spirit that lies beneath the assertion by many scientists and philosophers that there is no real conflict between science and religion. Stephen Jay Gould used the term "Nonoverlapping Magisteria" to suggest that science has nothing to say about religion, and *vice versa*.[12] This is false. As science continues to uncover explanations for phenomena in the natural world, supernatural explanations become less necessary, and certain religious myths no longer make sense. Many religious people are conflicted about this trend, and that seems appropriate; the conflict is perfectly real.

Religious dogmatism is just one of the anti-intellectual forces that scientists navigate. Scientific findings almost always make people uncomfortable or seem inconvenient if they contradict long held beliefs, have negative political ramifications, or threaten to cost people money. The same findings will be unconditionally accepted if they have the opposite effects, and a battle is joined. Particularly disturbing is the recent trend to introduce the television model of political point/counterpoint into public discussions of science. These discussions are not only unscientific; they can give the mistaken impression that there is an equivalence of legitimacy between the views being debated, which intentionally or not clouds the scientific issues. The debate over the causes of global climate change exemplifies the perfect storm where scientific results have important political and economic effects that play to existing partisan divides. Partisan supporters magnify marginal viewpoints in the public debate, and the net effect is to blur the distinction between science, on the one hand, and pseudoscience, opinion, faith, and political agendas, on the other. This is particularly damaging at a moment in history when scientific progress offers such tangible contributions to the betterment of the human condition.

This is the standard "not our fault" view of anti-intellectualism as seen from within the college and university culture. The notion is that the problems come from everyone else—politicians, the media, religious fundamentalists, and the failure of the K–12 system. Under the "not our fault" model, the academy is seen, at least by those that reside within the ivory tower, as the last bastion of intellectual purity in the midst of an increasingly savage and ignorant culture. This view has several problems. First, it is destructive. Second, it is itself anti-intellectual. Third, it fails to recognize the synergism between the academy and the outside world that has been the engine of technological advance in the United States over the last half century. Finally, it fails to recognize the anti-intellectual forces exerted by the academy, both internally (on itself), and externally (on society). I will consider each of these in turn.

US VERSUS THEM

Richard Hofstadter remarked that it was "ironic that the United States should have been founded by intellectuals, for throughout most of our political history, the intellectual has been for the most part either an outsider, a servant, or a scapegoat."[13] This "barbarian at the gates" sentiment is very common, but not particularly constructive. It portrays an isolated, self-righteous intellectual community that absolves itself of responsibility for the current state of affairs. Ironically, the term "anti-intellectual" is often used as an epithet, hurled by the more educated at the less educated, or as a derogatory term for someone who places undue priority on advancing commercial interests over social welfare.

Although it is a mistake to defend superstition and dogmatism in any form, it is unfair for academics to use a broad brush to paint business and economic interests as being purely anti-intellectual forces. The mutualism between the business world and the academic world has been the engine for the scientific and technological advances in western democracies.[14] The business world generates the national wealth that, primarily through the conduit of government, funds basic scientific research and intellectual advances in the social sciences and the humanities. In this arrangement, it is the job of the academic to educate, in both a vocational manner and in critical thinking, to generate a skilled workforce as well as a scientifically literate and socially responsible population.

Like mutualisms that exist within the biological world, the relationship between academics and the private sector is not without tension, especially if one side or the other is not honoring their part of the agreement. Intellectual horsepower and creativity are highly valued in the business world, but emphasis is placed on tangible (read: economic), short-term results. The academic community is more concerned with the unfettered advance of knowledge per se, with tangible benefits likely to come eventually, but too far in the future to be specifically predicted. Tensions rise when one community tries to project its priorities on the other. Hence, academics become concerned when educational or research priorities at colleges and universities are too closely connected to commercial interests or driven by development dollars. They feel that a greater fraction of the GDP should be dedicated to basic research. It is not that academics want to do useless research; it is that they understand the importance of unconstrained creativity, serendipitous discovery, and unanticipated applications. The public becomes concerned when a college education becomes disconnected from preparation for the workforce, or when research seems to have no tangible connection to the real world.

The goals of higher education therefore represent both a pure and applied science, the pure being the development of intellect and advancement of knowledge, and the applied being the acquisition of skills and credentials for economic, social, or personal advancement. Even within the sciences, the relationship between pure and applied research is generally the most tense because, despite their mutual interdependence, they have very different short-term priorities. Basic research is stimulating to some, but amounts to no practical benefit if it can never be applied, much less understood, outside the academy. Applied research would stagnate without advances in fundamental knowledge. To apply the mutualism analogy directly, the higher education system cannot respond to anti-intellectual pressures by isolating academics from relevance to society, nor can it continually pander to economic priorities, because each of these undermine its value to society. We must staunchly defend social investment in basic research and pure intellectual achievement. These are the unique elements of value that academics bring to the table in our mutualistic relationship with the private sector.

In intellectual circles, it is increasingly popular to blame anti-intellectual forces in politics, religion, business, and the media for the "dumbing down of America." But the perspective that Americans are anti-intellectual is no more intellectual than the view that intellectuals are anti-American. If one role of the university is to develop the national intellect, then we should take at least some responsibility for the current state of affairs. The first step in this process is to embrace the complex role that universities play in society, from purely intellectual development to training and economic advancement, but to have courage and stand ground when intellectual concerns take the back seat.

EXPRESS INTELLECTUAL COURAGE

If colleges and universities are going to pine for a more intellectual climate, then it is imperative to lead by example and address the anti-intellectual forces within the academy.

There are two major impediments to intellectual development. The first is being convinced that you always have the correct answer. The second is being convinced that there is no correct answer. Although these two viewpoints seem completely opposite, they have the same effect of discouraging inquiry.

The "*I have the answer*" syndrome is typical of religious and political dogmatism, and is the stereotypical anti-intellectualism Hofstadter described. It is also common in science education and hence the public understanding of science. Scientific theories change through time, starting out as one of several competing hypotheses and perhaps later being instantiated as fact (atomic theory, evolution, Copernican model of the solar system). Science is therefore a highly dynamic and creative (even artistic) process when hypotheses are observed aborning.

But this is seldom how science is portrayed in classes, where time is short and there is a priority placed on memorizing established fact. Science is damaged when viewed in this way. Gaps in knowledge are seen as weakness. Creationists often criticize evolutionary biology for having uncertainty about, say, the origins of a particular structure or of life itself. The distinction between theory and fact is often misunderstood by the general public and hence exploited by the opponents of science. "It's only a theory" is often used to assail the fact of evolution, though not used to discredit, for example, the aerofoil theory or the atomic theory of chemistry, because they do not contradict the book of Genesis. The result of these pressures, and a simple lack of time and effort, means the scientific uncertainties are glossed over and science is taught as facts to memorize. Consequently, most college and university graduates are not familiar with the scientific method, the creativity involved in developing scientific hypotheses and designing insightful experiments, standards of evidence and publication, or sometimes even the series of observations and experiments that led to the great discoveries they are being forced to memorize. This is hardly an intellectual endeavor.

The "there is no correct answer" syndrome is rooted from within the intellectual establishment, and has been taken to its extreme with cultural relativism, where everything can be viewed as a matter of perspective. At this extreme, there is no objective reality and therefore no objective truths. We see the pernicious effects of this philosophy in society when marginal theories become elevated as viable alternatives to established fact. The Intelligent Design (ID) movement is based on the interpretation that certain biological structures are simply too complex to have evolved, and so there must have been an intelligent designer. The movement is a cynical invention, careful to avoid the verbiage that the designer was God so that teaching ID in schools might pass judicial muster in a way that creationism could not.[15] This strategy has been soundly defeated in the courts but has been a resounding political success.[16] Part of this success comes from the creationism/ID movement borrowing the language of the intellectual: that people should be open-minded to any idea, no matter how bad. It was this purported openness of the religious community to any form of the creation myth that is so effectively satirized by the Church of the Flying Spaghetti Monster.[17] When former President George W. Bush was asked about his support for the teaching of ID in schools, he responded with the language of an intellectual: "Part of education is to expose people to different schools of thought. . . . You're asking me whether or not people ought to be exposed to different ideas, and the answer is yes."[18] I agree, provided the lesson concludes with the understanding that, regardless of your religious affinities, the ID movement has been repudiated as junk science.

The "there is no correct answer" syndrome is also what lies beneath the negative stereotype of the intellectual as indecisive, dawdling, and lacking in conviction. It is increasingly recognized that in the more extreme forms of cultural relativism, these stereotypes have some basis in fact. From the perspective of a scientist, a particularly irksome development is the invention of "scientism" as a pejorative term to suggest that science is a just another ideology that rationalizes Western societal norms. In this view, science is not a proven means to reveal objective facts about the natural world; rather, it is like any other religious movement.

> [Scientism is] the often quite fanatical belief in the omnipotence of the (mainly natural) sciences . . . it is a form of rationalism that fanatically fights all forms of ignorance—but that of religion in particular. While religious faith is defined as irrational ignorance, the rational sciences . . . are elevated to well nigh metaphysical heights. . . . The "god" of this rationalism nowadays is "the selfish gene," which is a late-modern specimen of predestination. Doubt as an intrinsic part of faith is, of course, always rejected by true believers—those whom we nowadays label "fundamentalists." . . . There is an interesting coalescence of scientism and religious fundamentalism in the ongoing debate between evolutionism and creationism.[19]

As a scientist, and a radical adherent to "scientism," I respond to the charge of omnipotence of the sciences with, "I wish." To the notion that science fights all forms of ignorance, I plead "Guilty as charged." However, it is inappropriate to portray evolution and creationism as a difference of opinion among opposing fundamentalists. Would it be scientific fundamentalism to staunchly defend the Copernican model of the solar system? There is no scientific debate about evolution, and any debate that exists in the public has nothing to do with the philosophy of science. This passage is simply a repackaging of the relativist notion that the advancement of scientific knowledge is just another anthropological system of social or even religious beliefs, with no special basis in objective reality. It clouds the distinction between scientific fact and theological opinion.

The culture of colleges and universities must balance intellectual openness with the fact that there is an objective reality and that some ideas are better than others. We have no problem rejecting astrology, or flying saucers, or the notion that masturbation gives you hairy palms. The hypothesis that Helios (later named Apollo) drove the chariot of the sun across the sky is now dismissed as a quaint myth. What exactly makes Helios an implausible supernatural being? Like the story in the Book of Genesis, the Helios myth runs contrary to science, but the validity of the Helios myth is not open for debate. In today's world Helios worshippers would have to reconcile their faith with the fact that the earth moves relative to the sun, and not vice versa. How, then, should we respond to the more than 40% of the U.S. population that believes in the scientifically discredited notion that the earth is less than 10,000 years old? One thing we should *not* do is portray the age of the earth as simply one point of view. What seems like a generous sentiment of tolerance for a diversity of perspectives breaks down when truth and fiction, reason and reaction, or science and pseudoscience are viewed as equally viable ways to think and learn about the world. One role of the intellectual community in our society is to explore the diversity of ideas, but we must also express some intellectual courage and contribute more substantively to the public discourse about which ideas are better than others and how to differentiate them.

In *Science as a Way of Knowing,* John Moore contrasts "the two dominant and antagonistic patterns of thought we have inherited—one based on the acceptance of supernatural forces, authority, or revelation to explain the phenomena of nature and another relying on observations, data, hypotheses, and verifiable conclusions."[20] Science is the voice of reason kept in tune by the weight of evidence. It is neither plausible nor desirable to make everything and everyone scientific, but an appreciation of reason and evidence as means to arrive at one's convictions is part of the basic skill set for an enlightened culture.

DEFEND SCIENCE AS A PUBLIC GOOD

An important distinction between science and religion is that, in the United States, at least, your religion is your own business. Scientific discoveries, however, are often public goods, meaning that the benefits of science are often accrued broadly, perhaps to all citizens. It is difficult for uncoordinated markets to produce public goods because there is little incentive for the production costs to be paid by individual entities if the benefits are accrued to others, including the so-called free-riders that choose not to invest. This is known as the public goods problem. There are several solutions to the problem of creating public goods, but the most relevant here is where beneficiaries agree to pool resources. Governments, for example, can be thought of as mechanisms for pooling resources by making contributions involuntary. Thus, individuals who do not value advances in certain areas of science will nevertheless contribute to their development. Thus, research in evolutionary biology, or tax advantages to faith-based organizations are supported by the tax dollars of creationists and atheists alike, as long as they are broadly construed as contributing to the public good.

Whether or not something is a public good can be difficult to determine precisely. In science, for example, applied research into factors that generate higher yield in corn would directly benefit companies that develop crops. Hence it pays those companies to fund such research, which they have successfully done. Ironically, the fundamental research in plant physiology, biochemistry, genetics, evolution, and ecology that combined to make those advances necessary were less likely to garner corporate investment because the payoffs were not directly related to their business. That research was not unimportant. In fact, the benefits of fundamental advances can be so broadly accrued that the research becomes a public good. This is why governmental agencies fund basic research at colleges and universities; such important research would not otherwise be conducted. Indeed, the 2009 Global Competitiveness Report from the World Economic Forum (WEF) credits the United States with having "the most competitive economy in the world" in large part due to its "excellent university system that collaborates strongly with the business sector in R&D."[21] Thus, the mutualism between pure and applied research described above is not merely beneficial; it is directly responsible for our standard of living.

The point is that our previous success resulted from a societal understanding that advances in basic science are public goods that merit collective investment. Despite that understanding, academics face non-intellectual pressures to pursue more applied or "translational" research (i.e., research of immediate clinical importance). University administrations want access to research dollars. Any corporation would directly benefit from a university system that shares its research agenda. Everyone wants advances in medicine. However, any emphasis away from basic research is a missed opportunity to advance the fundamental knowledge on which the advance of the private sector economy depends. In the face of these pressures, it is the job of university researchers and administrators to confidently defend basic research, and knowledge for the sake of knowledge, because it is their unique role in society to supply these public goods.

DEFEND EDUCATION AS A PUBLIC GOOD

Higher education is also a public good. When citizens are educated, some of the benefit accrues to us all and not just to those who receive the education. The creation of the land-grant college system in the 1860s, the development of universal primary and secondary schooling early in the 20th century, and the system of superior state universities amount to a tremendous societal investment in education. However, with funding for state universities dwindling and tuition rising, the signs are that our society increasingly sees higher education as a private good, with the benefit accruing primarily to the individual receiving it.[22] This has two important consequences. First, nobody is ever quite sure whom or what a college education is for (public good? private benefit?). Second, as education becomes an increasingly private good, institutions of higher education are driven by competitive market forces in attracting students and their families as customers.

The modern world of marketing higher education contributes to an anti-intellectual climate both inside and outside the academy. Just how anti-intellectual has college recruitment become? The following quotes are from a series of e-mails from an institution of higher learning:

> Dear J,
>   If you submit your Gold Crest Application by midnight tonight, I can still guarantee you the benefits I mentioned in my previous e-mails:
>
> - No application fee to pay
> - No new essay to write
> - A two-week admissions decision
>
>   Click here to finish your exclusive application to _____ College. This is the last day I can offer you this opportunity . . .
>
> Dear J,
>   I see that you didn't make yesterday's deadline. I'm so interested in seeing you apply to _____ College, I'm giving you until *midnight tonight* to finish and submit . . . During this *24-hour extension* . . .
>
> Dear J,
>   I have great news! Because I believe you could be a very special part of our next incoming class, I'm giving you more time . . . You now have until March 1 . . .

The objective observer could barely distinguish this transcript of a college advertisement from a late-night infomercial.

While marketing is a practical necessity for many institutions that struggle to fill classrooms with tuition-paying students, selective institutions also compete intensively for the best and brightest students.[23] This competition and entrepreneurial mentality has led to many improvements in student life; the food is better, the dorms are cleaner, there is broad access to state-of-the-art recreational facilities. But there are also many nefarious practices, most centered on the intense competition to move upward in the annual rankings such as those published by *U.S. News & World Report*.[24] Clemson University was accused of gaming the system by various means, including the assertion that the president's office consistently ranked other programs below average to improve its relative position (this charge was denied by the office of President James Barker).[25] Institutions of higher education urge alumni/ae to give $1 to increase the fraction of alumni/ae giving, or reclassify non-giving alumni/ae as deceased. There are discrepancies between the SAT scores reported to bond agencies, versus those reported by *U.S. News*, the latter generally being higher.[26] How much is the early decision process designed to enhance yield rate (the ratio of the number of students who choose to attend among those who were accepted)? How much of the marketing process is simply to increase the number of applications and hence "selectivity"?

As intensely as colleges and universities compete for the best students, students compete for admission. The culture of competitive admission, anti-intellectual practices, and the resulting tone of college admissions comes at an immense social cost. For many students, their entire academic and extracurricular lives are led with a clear eye to college admissions. Although a high GPA, class rank, AP classes, sports, the arts, community service, and so on are all great things, they are all too often done for the wrong reasons. Private school guidance offices and private counseling firms begin in the freshman year of high school to help choose summer activities or help you spin those experiences. For too many students, there is a seamless transition of these non-intellectual priorities into college, as students vie for admission to professional schools. For academic advisors, it is all too common to see 20-year-old students suffering from a decade of accumulated pressure, many lament living a life that is, up to that point, not one of their own choosing.

How can colleges and universities become more intellectual institutions, and project those intellectual priorities into our culture? To administrators, the market forces seem inexorable, with dire consequences for the university that stands alone in ignoring them. An important step would be to recognize that the institution does not exist solely for the benefit of its customers, and is at least to some extent a public good. This is true of both public and private institutions.

One place to start is with the notion that students are analogous to consumers in a private sector business, an attitude that instantiates the perspective that education is strictly a private good. Consider the very best students that attract full scholarships. They are not the best customers. They are students brought in to make the institution better. The Peace Corps is a government agency that recruits volunteers. It advertises and people apply. These volunteer employees are not referred to as customers because the Peace Corps is still in the business of providing a public good.

Once we accept the fact that a college education and the institutions of higher education themselves are in part a public good, we can recognize the rankings of *U.S. News* and our own aggressive marketing campaigns are anti-intellectual forces that damage them. That is an important step. Challenging the orthodoxy takes some courage unless you are the dominant market force and can drive the dynamics on your own. For example, some liberal arts colleges are making the SAT optional, and while one can debate whether this is a courageous stance against elements of standardized testing or a clever niche marketing ploy, these schools have seen a surge in minority applicants.[27] Early admission is increasingly used as a competitive tactic that extracts a commitment from prospective students for the veiled assurance of an increased probability of acceptance. Elite public universities such as Berkeley, Ann Arbor, and Chapel Hill are also in a uniquely powerful position to make these statements because a combined mission that includes service to the state is an explicit portion of their mission. Colleges and universities could also act together. If the higher education establishment truly resents the oversimplification and pernicious effects of the rankings by *U.S. News*, how difficult would it be for leading institutions to work publicly on metrics upon which they would like students to base their college decisions? Even a reasoned discussion of what these metrics should be, and how they would vary for students with different needs, would be a welcome change toward a more intellectual culture.

The American college and university system is seen as the world leader in basic research and intellectual development. If this is true, then these institutions must accept some responsibility for the current state of affairs. In particular, we must oppose anti-intellectual forces within the academy, and project intellectual ideals into the culture at large. There is a growing urgency for colleges and universities to do what they do best: generate pure knowledge and capture the imaginations of the brightest minds. Rather than insulate themselves from what they might perceive as the barbarians at the gate, or compromise their investment in basic research, academic institutions should purposefully engage the private sector and promote our system of higher education as a public good that is worthy of societal investment.

NOTES

1. Snapping shrimp are finger-sized marine animals, so named because they have one large claw that when snapped shut emits the loudest sound in the ocean. The sound, used to momentarily stun their prey, is not generated from the claw itself, but from the intense pressure exerted on miniscule air bubbles, generating light, heat, and intense sound.

2. Norman R. Augustine, Chair, *Is America Falling off the Flat Earth?* (Washington, DC: The National Academies Press, 2007), 42.

3. Frank Newport, "Republicans, Democrats Differ on Creationism," http://www.gallup.com/poll/108226/republicans-democrats-differ-creationism.aspx

4. Augustine, *Is America Falling off the Flat Earth?*; George M. Whitesides, Chair, *Rising Above the Gathering Storm: Energizing and Employing America for a Brighter Economic Future* (Washington, DC: National Academies Press, 2007).

5. Celia W. Dugger, "Study Cites Toll of AIDS policy in South Africa," *New York Times*, November 25, 2008.

6. Richard Hofstadter, *Anti-Intellectualism in American Life* (New York: Knopf, 1963); Susan Jacoby, *The Age of American Unreason* (New York: Pantheon, 2008).

7. Jacoby, *The Age*, 252.

8. Augustine, *Is America Falling off the Flat Earth?*, 32.

9. Ibid., 32.

10. Whitesides, *Rising Above the Gathering Storm*, 31.

11. There are some signals that U.S. dominance in higher education might be starting to change. Rankings of U.S. institutions are particularly vulnerable to assessments where the sciences are given relatively heavy emphasis. See Scott Jaschik, "US Decline or a Flawed Measure?" *Inside Higher Ed*, October 8, 2009, http://www.insidehighered.com

12. Stephen Jay Gould, "Nonoverlapping Magisteria," *Natural History* 106 (March 1997): 16–22.

13. Hofstadter, *Anti-Intellectualism*, 145–146.

14. "Mutualism" is a biological term: two very different agents interact with each other to gain mutual benefits. Coral reefs are built on the mutualism between colonies of animals (corals) and algae (called zooxanthellae) that reside within them. Zooxanthellae photosynthesize and in return for a safe place to live, transfer energy to their animal hosts in the form of sugars (such as glucose). Coral animals often supplement their glucose diet by catching animal prey. When the prey are digested, some of the nitrogen and other nutrients are passed on to the zooxanthellae as the raw materials for photosynthesis, and the arrangement is mutually beneficial. Zooxanthellae also give corals their color, which is why corals turn white (so-called coral bleaching) when the mutualism is lost. But mutualisms are often filled with tension, and difficult to sustain when one or the other partner does not play its part. A major hypothesis for the cause of coral bleaching is that when water temperature increases (due, e.g., to El Niño or global warming), the photosynthetic machinery of the zooxanthellae deteriorates to such a point that the coral hosts expel their mutualists. It is, in human parlance, a case of "what have you done for me lately?"

15. In the landmark case, *Kitzmiller vs. Dover Area School Distinct*, U.S. District Court Judge John E. Jones III ruled that the teaching of Intelligent Design (ID) in the schools was unconstitutional. The opinion is a lucid and thorough repudiation of ID, concluding it is a version of creationism and definitively not science. I refer to the movement as cynical because the defendants were clearly found to be misrepresenting their motivations, attempting in vain to distance themselves from creationism to the point of giving untruthful testimony. The religious motivations of the ID movement were made especially clear when it was found that the ID text, *Of Pandas and People: The Central Question of Biological Origins*, had undergone systematic revision where more than 100 references to creationism were replaced with the phrases referring to Intelligent Design.

John Stewart quipped that ID proponents are "not saying it's God, just someone with the basic skill set to create an entire universe" (*The Daily Show*, Evolution Schmevolution Series, Comedy Central, September 2005).

16. While Americans oppose creationism on equal footing with science (Susan Jacoby, *Freethinkers: A History of American Secularism* [New York: Henry Holt, 2005], 362), the majority of the public sees no problem placing intelligent design on an equal footing (Harris Interactive, "Nearly Two-thirds of U.S. Adults Believe Human Beings Were Created by God," Harris Poll #52, July 6, 2005). It is a successful campaign to blur the distinction between scientific and religious concepts.

17. Church of the Flying Spaghetti Monster, www.venganza.org

18. Peter Baker and Peter Slevin, "Bush Remarks on 'Intelligent Design' Theory Fuel Debate," *Washington Post*, August 3, 2005.

19. Peter Berger and Anton Zijderveld, *In Praise of Doubt: How to Have Convictions without Becoming a Fanatic* (New York: HarperCollins Publishers, 2009), 102–103.

20. John A. Moore, *Science as a Way of Knowing* (Cambridge, MA: Harvard University Press, 1993).

21. David R. Butcher, "2009 Global R&D Outlook," www.thomasnet.com

22. Whitesides, *Rising Above the Gathering Storm*, 31.

23. David L. Kirp, *Shakespeare, Einstein, and the Bottom Line: The Marketing of Higher Education* (Cambridge, MA: Harvard University Press, 2003).

24. Ibid., 25–30.

25. Doug Lederman, "The Best University?" *Inside Higher Ed*, June 9, 2009, http://www.insidehighered.com

26. Kirp, *Shakespeare, Einstein, and the Bottom Line*, 25–30.

27. Ibid., 31.

CHAPTER 3

Liberated Consumers and the Liberal Arts College

Elaine Tuttle Hansen

In his address to the joint session of Congress on February 24, 2009, President Obama announced the vision intended to change the landscape of higher education in the United States. By 2020, he proclaimed, "America will once again have the highest proportion of college graduates in the world." "College" is loosely defined in this mandate—"This can be community college or a four-year school; vocational training or an apprenticeship."[1] The pronouncement focuses welcome attention on the importance of postsecondary education, but to implement such broad aspirations, we now need a national conversation not only about issues of access, funding, and quality, but also, and more fundamentally, about purposes.

Currently there is no common understanding of why we need to provide higher education for more Americans, or what a better system would achieve. Is it about jobs or happiness, skills or knowledge, attitude or values, individual accomplishment or the common weal or the nation's global competitiveness? Amid the messiness and sprawl that is public discourse about education today, we hear mostly about test scores and accountability and cost. The situation remains as Patricia Albjerg Graham described it 25 years ago in her essay "Schools: Cacophony about Practice, Silence about Purpose," where she argued that "We Americans, who are appropriately vociferous in our critiques of education generally and the schools particularly, need to come to fundamental agreement about what we want our schools to do."[2] More recently, Anthony Bryk, president of the Carnegie Foundation for the Advancement of Teaching, has attributed some of the failures of our educational system to this same clamor of voices debating practices and policies and silent on the question of purposes.[3]

In at least one sector of higher education today, however, we find both clarity of purpose and a reasonable consensus about what excellence in achieving that purpose looks like: the small, residential, selective liberal arts colleges. Uniquely American, largely founded in the 18th and 19th centuries, liberal arts colleges are free-standing, residential, predominantly private institutions where the majority of students are full-time, traditional-aged undergraduates taught mostly by tenure-track or otherwise long-term and full-time faculty members, who offer curricular breadth, depth, and exploration in the evolving disciplines and interdisciplines of the arts, humanities, languages, natural sciences and mathematics, and social sciences. President Obama is a prime example of the successful outcomes of this educational experience. He started his own undergraduate career at one of these institutions, Occidental College, and then completed it at a research university that also houses one of the most traditional core liberal arts programs, at Columbia College.

For as long as I have paid attention to such matters, the liberal arts college sector has been said to be on the "endangered" list, embedded in what has been called "one or another narrative of decline," shrinking in numbers and/or in danger of losing its way.[4] In part this shift reflects the post–World War II expansion of other sectors as much as a modest (but difficult to measure accurately) decrease in the absolute number of institutions that might reasonably be classified as liberal arts colleges. Nonetheless, it is indisputable that in many regions and among many social groups, these institutions are largely invisible and irrelevant to the vast majority of the higher-education-seeking population. In conversations I have had with educational reformers, moreover, what liberal arts colleges do well tends to be quickly set aside as best practice, but not "scalable" to larger institutions and whole systems, and therefore unavailable to our most poorly served students. More outright critics conflate all liberal arts colleges (and often research universities as well) and take them to task for high costs, hoarded resources, unproven claims to excellence, and patently elitist practices (like "cream-skimming").[5] The economic recession tends to exacerbate such attacks. And even the staunchest practitioners and defenders of the liberal arts model see internal problems. For example, Haverford professor Kim Benston has suggested, "As we [liberal arts colleges] have grown in *purposive complexity*, so have we thrived, becoming . . . increasingly meritocratic, pluralistic, and just plain interesting; but as we have mimed the modern university's drift toward internal fragmentation and corporate simulation, we have courted a disquieting, and disabling, incoherence."[6]

It is also salient to note that this oldest and smallest sector of the American higher education landscape is not a homogeneous or even aptly named category. Viewed up close, there are significant material differences in the size, selectivity, national or regional reputation, and financial resources of liberal arts colleges. Each has, and for marketing purposes cultivates, a more or less differentiated identity. Like the complexity within each institution, these differences between liberal arts colleges lead to fragmentation and incoherence in the sector. Yet another particularly confounding aspect of this sector is the misnomer problem. Although it bears a venerable heritage, today the term "liberal arts" could hardly be a more unfortunate descriptor, troubled by multiple and misleading connotations of the words "liberal" and "arts," made fuzzier by the recent rise of the phrase "liberal education," and absent any semantic signal of what really differentiates these institutions as a sector.[7] Even without its negative associations, the term fails to capture their most constitutive characteristics, including the limited size and age-range of the undergraduate community; the small classroom experience and the close faculty-student relationship; the residential character of student life; the typical location on a single historic and aesthetically unified campus, only rarely situated in an urban area; and origin stories of founders (often religious) that live on today in the affective, values-laden aspect of their missions.

It is tempting to suggest that the so-called liberal arts colleges today might better be described as the "Quad and Lab" or "White Chapel and Green Lawn" or "Beds, Books and Beyond" Colleges. But no label I can imagine offers a serious alternative, and I do not mean to make light of this issue, because it has significant implications. In the past, "college" for the minority who were able to attend was more or less synonymous with the liberal arts college experience today; now the term has lost or seriously compromised its original meaning. Even as we seek to make higher education available to the vast majority of Americans, our language for explaining the options is thus impoverished, making clear thinking and strategic action all the more difficult. For example, many individual students who should be making more informed choices and lack good guidance may erroneously think that if they are interested in natural sciences and mathematics they cannot choose a liberal "arts" institution. The misnomer issue raises concerns as well as for setting reasonable and effective national policy. We need to know what we mean and who we are counting when we talk about things like having the highest proportion of college graduates in the world.

At the same time—despite the narratives of decline, the incoherence within and between the institutions in this sector, and the misnomer problem—there are strong counterindications to suggest that the liberal arts college model, which dates back to the earliest days of European settlement in this country, has far from run its course or outlived its value. The popularity of the most prestigious liberal arts colleges is higher than ever within a certain small strata of society, especially among the most highly educated. Two of the elite service academies have recently adopted the liberal arts classification. Other nations (especially now in Asia) aspiring to improve their own educational systems are studying the way our liberal arts colleges do it. Holding the line against the forces of the "multiversity," liberal arts colleges frequently outperform research universities and other larger institutions in quantitative measures like retention and graduation rates and postgraduate study. They create the only conditions in which faculty can fully realize the mutually enriching synthesis of teaching and research.[8] Growing strength and accessibility can be demonstrated by trends in selectivity (the percentage of applicants accepted, which has been in many cases shrinking), yield (the percentage of admitted students who decide to enroll, which has been increasing), and discount rate (a measure of expenditures on financial aid, which has also been intentionally and in some cases dramatically increasing). Parents and students vote with their feet to support liberal arts colleges not only by paying high tuition but also by contributing to the annual funds and endowments that allow many institutions today to sustain, among other things, those rapidly rising financial aid budgets.[9]

As we tackle the challenges of aspiring to "college for all," assuming we do not want to tolerate mediocrity at best, with failure the more likely outcome, I propose taking a closer look at what we can learn from considering both the strengths and weaknesses of these models of undergraduate educational excellence in the United States, the liberal arts colleges. In what follows, I discuss first the mission and supporting practices of this sector. Before concluding, I will also consider some of the troubling challenges that confront the liberal arts colleges today, but in the end I reiterate my main premise: liberal arts colleges are the leaders and standard bearers of American higher education; their purposes have never been clearer, more distinct, or more relevant to both individual and public well-being; and this small sector therefore offers us a "vanguard" model, with both sustainable and adaptable features that are pertinent to any discussion of the purposes of higher education in the 21st century.[10]

THE LIBERATING LIBERAL ARTS

If my premise that the purposes of liberal arts colleges have never been more distinctive, effective, and relevant to individual and collective well-being has merit, then why is their "value proposition" clear to only a small percentage of Americans today, and so poorly understood or accepted by the vast majority? There are many ways of explaining this situation, and I will talk about more of them later when I explore a few of the most intractable challenges for the liberal arts sector today. But one important reason to acknowledge is our failure to translate the intangible, perhaps even ineffable aims of our educational model into terms that touch directly on the concrete and pressing needs of both individuals and society today. The vagueness and abstraction of our purposes is reflected in the published mission statements of most liberal arts colleges. And this situation confounds even our most passionate and loyal fans, as I learned when I became the chief explicating officer of a liberal arts college. Many trustees and alumni/ae who are living examples of the successful outcomes of the educational experience we provide are frustrated by their own inability to capture and communicate their lived knowledge, their deep conviction, in words that they find adequate and persuasive. As anyone who tries to do so will attest, it is especially difficult to come up with a single catchphrase that grabs busy people with limited attention spans and very little patience for subtle and complicated prose, something that penetrates and resonates in the era of sound bites and tweets.

So it is with the hope of grabbing attention, frankly, that I want to suggest another, perhaps striking and possibly shocking way of articulating the ultimate value and purpose of a liberal arts education. We prepare people to be what I suggest the world most desperately needs to ensure a better future for most of its citizens: *liberated consumers.*

I choose the word "liberated" to tap into one of the root ideas of the "liberal" arts: that they represent the capacities needed to be a free human being, not servile, not enslaved either literally or figuratively. The word has some local resonance for me as well, since the college I presided over for 9 years was founded by abolitionists; its first president traveled south, after the Civil War, to recruit ex-slaves. And one of our most distinguished graduates in the early 20th century was Benjamin Mays, the youngest of eight children of former slaves, who grew up in South Carolina and first earned the right to vote in 1945 when he was 51 years old. Mays graduated from Bates in 1920, completed his Ph.D. at the University of Chicago, was dean of Howard University's School of Religion, became the first African American president of the Atlanta Board of Education, and for 27 years served as president of Morehouse College, where he first began his mentorship of Martin Luther King, Jr. Mays' most succinct testimony to the effectiveness of his liberal arts education appears in his autobiography, *Born to Rebel* (1971): "Bates College did not 'emancipate' me; it did the far greater service of making it possible for me to emancipate myself, to accept with dignity my own worth as a free man."

A century and a half after slavery was abolished, 90 years after Mays' graduation from Bates, 50 years after *Brown v. Board of Education,* we might well ask what "greater service" higher education owes its students today. From and to what do we need to "emancipate" all young people? In his book *Consumed: How Markets Corrupt Children, Infantilize Adults, and Swallow Citizens Whole,* Benjamin Barber offers one compelling possibility when he describes our current enslavement to "an ethos of induced childishness: an infantilization that is closely tied to . . . our radical consumerist society today." As consumers, according to Barber's argument, we are incapable of joining in the enterprise of making difficult "public choices" about social goods, in the context of real constraints; we lack a sense of agency and adult selfhood; we do not accept our worth or act with dignity as free human beings or in Barber's words "moral being[s] embedded in a free community."[11] The urgency of educating more liberated consumers is thrown into relief by the global economic crisis. As Matt Miller observes in *The Tyranny of Dead Ideas*, "We've overestimated the individual's control; we've felt entitled to 'more' and become disillusioned at its absence; and we've grown addicted to debt-fueled consumption."[12]

In proposing that the purpose of education is the emancipation of students from the shackles of a consumerist society, and thus to produce what I call "liberated consumers," I use the word "consumer" in a sense intended to summon up and interrogate its negative connotations. To say we live today in a consumerist society is to state the obvious. No single one of us can avoid being a consumer in the broadest sense; each individual is consuming all the time, in order to exist. At the same time, the most pressing collective issues of our day turn on questions about how to support and manage our massive aggregate needs for consumption—of food, of natural resources, of information—and the social, public consequences of human consumption that are sometimes so difficult to see, always complicated to understand, and seemingly impossible to control.

As individuals it is necessary, and seductive, to be focused on our personal consumption and our private choices. But as a society we see with growing urgency the necessity of making better collective choices about what and how we consume, despite the challenges of doing so without inequities and trade-offs. What I propose to call the "liberated consumer" (which we might also think of as the "citizen consumer" or the "conscious consumer" or, as a colleague recently suggested, the "mindful consumer") is no more and no less than someone who does not think she is free from the necessity of consuming—she is maybe even someone who likes to shop—but does not want to succumb to the pressure to consume mindlessly and ubiquitously.

It is worth noting that Barber does not view higher education today as a meaningful part of the effort to overcome the problems he identifies. "Colleges and universities that once acted as a counterpoint to commercial culture today," he rails, "have gone prostrate before corporate sponsors of research that academic administrators have neither the will nor the independent funding to oppose. Higher education has always been prone to the forces of vocationalism," Barber adds, but "today's new higher ed corruption comes from treating students themselves not as autonomous learners but as free consumers and not yet committed brand-shoppers."[13] Yet at another point he also notes, "Liberty understood as the capacity to make public choices . . . is a potential faculty that must be learned rather than a natural one that is exercised from birth. . . . It points to the core meaning now lost to most educational institutions in America of public schooling in the 'liberal arts.' The liberal arts are the arts of liberty necessary to the exercise of citizenship in a free republic."[14]

I by no means wish to propose that attending a liberal arts college is the only way to become a liberated consumer (or to study what is normally thought of as the liberal arts today). Individuals in all walks of life, with all kinds of educational backgrounds, are engaged in efforts to free themselves from the "induced childishness" of our consumerist society and from the addiction to craving more things that can never, by definition, be satisfied. But at liberal arts colleges today, some common practices and principles directly and intentionally and in a highly integrated way support this mission of preparing liberated consumers. Let me first list and then say a few words about each of these characteristic and closely interrelated elements:

- Calling students to *complexity*, *difficulty*, and relative *slowness* (as opposed to choosing what is simple, easy, and fast).
- Related to complexity, difficulty, and slowness: cultivating greater capacity to *focus* in a world of "continuous partial attention."
- Privileging *production* (of ideas), *participation* (in knowledge-making), making and doing and being proactive as opposed to passive spectatorship and the busy work of consuming goods and services manufactured by others, or craving and addiction to more.
- Learning in close-knit but not closed communities of practice, where emphasis is placed on (1) sustaining *friendship* and human connections as opposed to relationships with brand as substitute for human interaction, and (2) seeing the self as part of something bigger.
- Embracing *contradictions.*

Calling students to complexity, difficulty, and relative slowness (as opposed to what is simple, easy, and fast).[15] The value of the academic rigor and challenge that liberal arts colleges are able to promote, thanks to small classes of motivated students taught by scholars dedicated to undergraduate teaching, cannot be overestimated in the educational preparation of liberated consumers. The curricular experience at liberal arts colleges is designed to engage students positively and intentionally with appropriate levels of complexity and difficulty early on. Faculty have higher expectations than ever, and students not only select for themselves courses in areas they know nothing about but normally fulfill variously mandated or advisor-promoted "requirements" inside and outside their major fields of study, which direct them to a broad range of subjects and progressive levels of difficulty. At the same time, holding students to high academic standards and introducing them to unfamiliar and difficult materials go hand in hand with giving them ample support and structured as well as unscripted opportunities to try multiple paths, to venture into the unknown, to experiment and fail and start over as well as to rise to new levels of success.

To allow for an intense, demanding courseload that develops intellectual breadth, depth, and daring, the liberal arts college model has historically followed the "time out" model, preferring a slower, more thoughtful progress that stands in contrast to the frantic pace and constant distraction that we now regard as normal and irreversible. But as a liberal arts college alumnus and trustee recently said to me, the college experience should really be called "time in"—marking a period of years when young people are allowed to immerse themselves in learning and to journey inward, finding out who they are and what they love to do. Whether conceived of as time in or time out, this is an old educational idea—a century ago Alfred North Whitehead observed, "The initial discipline of imagination in its period of youthful vigour requires that there be no responsibility for immediate action. The habit of unbiased thought . . . cannot be acquired when there is the daily task for preserving a concrete organisation. You must be free to think rightly and wrongly, and free to appreciate the variousness of the universe undisturbed by its perils."[16] Unlike much that we experience, a liberal arts education is not about the bottom line or the short term; it is not about doing things faster or cheaper or even necessarily (and certainly not immediately) solving today's problems as much as it is about being in it for the long haul and doing the right thing.

Related to complexity, difficulty and slowness, cultivating greater capacity for focus in a world of "continuous partial attention." As David Brooks writes, "Control of attention is the ultimate individual power."[17] Or as David Foster Wallace put it, the issue is "how to exercise some control over how and what you think."[18] Two of the oldest pedagogical strategies common to all disciplines and programs at liberal arts colleges deepen this capacity for focus and control: encouraging more listening and emphasizing better questioning. Both are skills to be exercised first, before we demand answers, to enhance attentiveness and concentration.

Listening is a powerful and difficult skill, and above all learning how to listen to what is unfamiliar or disturbing to received opinion and commonly understood ways of thinking should be essential to many kinds of higher education. To develop advanced listening skills, liberal arts colleges encourage what we might call "incendiary listening"—listening that may inflame and illumine. Students are asked to walk into their classrooms, their dorms, or the dining halls and other gathering spaces where they repeatedly come together expecting that at any moment they might hear something that will change their lives, or at least spark some new insight. And they are encouraged to listen to themselves, too–to reflect on what they deeply know and truly care about, what they hear when they are able to block out noise and concentrate on what is often thought of as the inner voice.

The companion skill to listening is asking questions, and a liberal arts college experience demands that students learn to deploy various types of questions, all of which further focus the attention. The process of developing the capacity to question everything may begin by emphasizing open-ended questions. (At some colleges, this is signaled even before matriculation by requiring a supplement to the common application, for example, where we ask applicants to write in response to a two-word prompt for self-reflection: "Why Bates?") Once enrolled, students find that discussion is the signature pedagogy of the liberal arts college, and they are encouraged to respond to and use open-ended questions to get conversations started and perhaps especially to broach difficult issues, where there is likely to be conflict: "So from your perspective, what's happening in the Middle East? Why do you think that?" Probing questions further exercise the capacity to focus, and students learn to ask these kinds of questions of themselves and of the authority figures they encounter, too: "Can you say more? Can you help me understand what that means? How do you explain the counterevidence?" And *big* questions are perhaps the best known staple of a liberal arts education. Students in late adolescence need little prompting to interrogate themselves as well as teachers, experts, and peers: "Who am I? What do I love to do? How can I make a difference in the world?" Questioning the question, finally, is valued and encouraged. As one graduating senior told me, when I asked him one of these "big questions," "If four years . . . has taught me anything, it has taught me to be critical and to look long and hard at the question before even beginning to formulate an answer."

Privileging production (of ideas), participation (in knowledge making and sharing), making and doing, and being proactive as opposed to passive spectatorship and the busy work of consuming goods and services manufactured by others, or craving and addiction to more. Experiential learning in the lab, embodied learning in the arts or athletics, service learning and civic engagement–these and many other curricular and extra-curricular pursuits of students at liberal arts colleges today are all equally and deeply integral to our mission. Liberal arts colleges have the capacity to embrace and support these extended ways of learning because of their small size and, above all, their residential nature. The emphasis on making and doing in all spaces of endeavor, not replacing but extending the reach of the classroom and supervised academic work, is especially effective in breaking down unproductive preconceptions about the differences between work and play. As Dutch philosopher Johan Huizinga argued decades ago in *Homo Ludens*, what distinguishes human beings as a species is our playful nature, our innate curiosity, our love of competition, and our readiness to be diverted and distracted. Just as individual human beings must play as children in order to develop intellectually, socially, and emotionally, so too everything important about civilization—ritual, poetry, music and dance, war and politics—grows out of play, yet never outgrows play in its most critical dimensions.[19] More recently Dr. William Gaver, professor of Interaction Research at the Royal College of Art, puts it thus: "Play is not just mindless engagement, but an essential way of engaging with and learning about our world and ourselves, for adults as well as children. As we toy with things and ideas, as we chat and daydream, we find new perspectives and new ways to create, new ambitions, relationships, and ideas. Play goes well beyond entertainment; it is serious business."[20]

An undergraduate once said to me that his education involved not exactly seeing that the lines between work and play are blurred, but rather learning to distinguish between "simple play," on the one hand, and the satisfaction, the joy even, that he had taken from the hard work he had done in college, on the other. As another student added, if the enjoyment of academic work is anything like play, it is like chess. It is this sense of play, then—not the mindlessness of spectatorship and consuming the productions and performances of others, but the rare moments and activities when we feel caught up in something that we would do whether anyone paid us or not—that the liberal arts college aims to make possible for an extended period of time, inside and around the classroom and through formal and informal participation in experience for which the label "extracurricular" is another impoverished term.

Learning in communities of practice and sustaining friendship and human connections as opposed to relationships with brand as substitute for human interaction, where self is part of something bigger. Perhaps nothing about a liberal arts college education is more distinctive and critical or less examined and theorized than the residential backdrop, the oddly neglected or taken-for-granted fact that we still plunge perfect young strangers—now increasingly from all over the country and the world—into the most intimate proximity, and then demand the simultaneous development of both interpersonal skills and collective priorities by asking them to live together in these close, often self-maintained and regulated communities for several years. Again, Wallace vigorously affirms one key educational principle behind residential experience and the lifelong capacity for relationships it notoriously creates: "And I submit that this is what the really, no-bull value of your liberal arts education is supposed to be about: How to keep from going through your comfortable, prosperous, respectable adult life dead, unconscious, a slave to your head and to your natural default-setting of being uniquely, completely, imperially alone, day in and day out."[21]

There are too many dimensions to this powerful educational practice to do justice to them here; out of residential life come many types and modes of experiences that build individual and social capacity. Some involve casual, fluid relationships that may last for the space of a shared activity. In addition to the obvious benefits—like honing the ability to work in groups, often with people of different backgrounds and perspectives—such experiences support a vaguer feeling or atmosphere of "friendliness" on the liberal arts campus that gives content and value to otherwise abstract ideas of community and creates conditions that can counter the negative side of intense competition. Students in residence at liberal arts colleges also have abundant opportunities to develop with a few of their peers those deep and enduring relationships that we value so highly, and that some believe are increasingly threatened by new forms of social networking.

But residential living at its very best is about more, even, than lifelong friendships. As one recent teaching experience reminded me, voluntary association in and responsibility to a group can facilitate the growth of vital intellectual tools that offer alternatives to what we call "critical thinking," even as this kind of participation exercises the capacity to think about self as a "moral being embedded in a free community." In an advanced expository writing class offered to a small group of undergraduates a few years ago, I asked students to work with Peter Elbow's *Writing Without Teachers*, a well-known book laying out both philosophical arguments and practical steps that challenge traditional ways of teaching writing. Elbow's work is perhaps most frequently associated with the concept of freewriting, but there is another less familiar step in his recommended process that comes after freewriting and before editing—sharing a draft with a group of other people, readers who are *not* "teachers," in the traditional sense of the term, but are in fact better able to help a writer understand how to do the hardest part of writing, "getting things inside someone else's head."[22] The readers in the group at this stage must work hard not to point out what's right and wrong, but rather to describe what they experience as they read. The writer in turn must work hard to accept just about everything readers say as though it were all true. In fact, the reactions that seem craziest or most stupid may be the very most useful ones, because those are the perceptions the writer has been incapable of having. Writers must train themselves to listen openly, take it all in, and only then decide what to do next to improve their own thinking and thereby reach others more effectively.

Elbow's teacherless method, for both writers and readers who form a purposive voluntary group, rests on what he calls "the believing game," best understood as the complement and opposite of critical thinking, which he dubs "the doubting game." Critical thinking, a wonderful intellectual tool and major cornerstone (if not cliché) of a liberal arts education, requires us to look for the error in each assertion, using the highly serviceable tools of debate, critique, and argument. It also asks us to hold what we often refer to as our subjectivity—our wishes, preconceptions, experiences, and commitments—to one side. (As Elbow points out, we have developed more tools, like "the machinery of symbolic logic," to help people with this part of the doubting game.[23])

The believing game follows different rules. It requires us to gather as many assertions as we can and then to assume provisionally that each might be true; we consider each one on its own merits, and we don't ask them to contend with one another. To this end, the believing game has a deeply social dimension. It works best to find and test ideas when "we make use of a group and have a disciplined method," one that entails "harnessing the resources of the group to try to see the maximum number of benefits or advantages of each proposal in turn." "Sometimes we can't see the weaknesses of an idea or proposal by simply looking for weaknesses," Elbow notes; "the weaknesses don't show up until we look for strengths in competing ideas."[24]

In order to appreciate the strengths of each proposal fully, we must try to share the experience of the person who brought it forward, and this requires "not an act of self-extrication, but an act of self-insertion, self-involvement—an act of projection."[25] The doubting game often leaves us stuck in our own mental frame of reference, Elbow observes; because it "invites people merely to criticize ideas they don't like, it permits them to stay insulated against any experience of alternative thinking."[26] The believing game forces us out of our original frame of reference, especially if we entertain the most radically different ideas—again, those "which at first may appear odd or threatening . . . at the limits of what we can imagine or explain."[27] After we have looked at the world through the lens of multiple competing proposals and seen the strengths and weaknesses of as many divergent ideas as possible, we are better equipped to move back to judgment and develop a rigorous argument in support of the proposal we believe to be most trustworthy and valid.[28]

Let me underscore, if it is not completely obvious, how we can connect the value of the believing game with our understanding of how and why "friendship" and close interaction among the increasingly diverse groups that inhabit liberal arts campuses today are essential keys to the education of liberated consumers, and to educational excellence in general. Whereas the doubting game, as Elbow says, is a great tool even when we are all alone, the complementary believing game can only work in a group that brings together people with the broadest possible differences who are nonetheless committed to a common intellectual task. The believing game mirrors the experience of the liberal arts college, offering 4 years in the company of peers all pursuing and accepting responsibility for the same private end—their own individual intellectual advancement—but in a context that invites and encourages them to move frequently outside their own mental frame of reference, to enter into alien ideas on the assumption that there is something to be learned from the perspective that seems the most divergent from one's own. Self is embedded in this context and through this process in that sense of belonging and responsibility to "something bigger"—a residential unit, an affinity group, a campus community, a historic institution, a region, a country, a world that needs thoughtful citizens and liberated consumers.

Embracing contradictions. Held in loose association by an overarching idea like educating the liberated consumer, the purposes of a liberal arts college education need not be reduced to a single end; in fact, they will remain multiple and diverse and often even contradictory. I have already alluded to a number of these familiar contradictions, and to sum up let me underscore how the liberal arts college mission holds in creative tension oppositions such as these: the curricular vs. the co-curricular, academic intensity vs. "friendliness," success vs. failure, vocationalism vs. "learning for its own sake," and private gain vs. public good.

First, *curricular vs. extracurricular:* As I have said, the educational experience offered by the residential liberal arts college today resists any clear opposition between the academic curriculum and the many activities that in more conventional thinking about education fall under the heading of cocurricular or extracurricular. What happens in the classroom and what happens outside the classroom are not the same, but they are deeply linked by among other things a prevailing drive toward high achievement and passionate pursuit in any realm. The voices of some liberal arts college students continue to punctuate this and other points: as one student recently told me, "I haven't met many people here who settle for halfway measures."

Next, *academic intensity vs. "friendliness":* At the same time, this sense of passionate focus and intensity is balanced and sustained by its own opposite, too—namely, the occupation of space for play and "social life" and the "aura of laid-backness," as another student put it, that marks the best liberal arts colleges. In the liberal arts college community, for this space of time at least, something as ordinary as the friendship and mutual respect between people is not incidental but essential to extraordinary scholarship and discovery. Students are more likely to compete with themselves, not others, on this kind of campus; at its best, a caring camaraderie encourages them to try the new and the difficult, to bite off more than elsewhere might seem possible to chew. Contacts with adult members of the community also—staff members as well as faculty, from the admissions officers to workers at Dining Services, from the librarians to the custodians—reinforce this sense that it is the people we live with who make it safe to take risks. This is yet another point at which we can meet one of higher education's greatest challenges—diversity and inclusion—with strategies that have wider application, because friendliness in this sense doesn't mean bland harmony and contentment. Rather, it means practicing the difficult art of respectful discord, and again risk-taking. As one student affirmed, "Differences of opinion are welcomed and the risk of making mistakes is respected, so long as you own them and learn from them."

Supporting and encouraging students to take risks also means blurring the boundaries between *success vs. failure.* Sometimes this means learning from mistakes, and being willing to try and try again. The redefinition of success and failure also permits persistence in an activity for the love of it—in the most profound sense of "amateur"—even for individuals who aren't the "stars." Another student recently spoke to me about the value of learning to play both a musical instrument and a sport that he had not attempted before coming to college. In 4 years he hadn't become quite proficient enough to play in the orchestra and had never been a starting player for the team, but "Where else," he said, "would I have been not just allowed but encouraged to do something not because I was going to be a star, but because I loved to do it and I was here to learn and stretch?"

Vocationalism/instrumentalism vs. "learning for its own sake": Perhaps the most irreconcilable contradiction in everyday thinking about the purposes of higher education today—heightened in the current economic moment, and reflected in President Obama's use of the term "college" to mean everything from a traditional 4-year bricks-and-mortar experience to a year of vocational training—turns on the question of utility. Are we training students for more successful careers, or are we cultivating more learned minds for the sheer joy of learning? Like the tension between academics and extracurricular activities, this long-lived debate simply evaporates when you listen to liberal arts college students and watch their performance on the job market. "Learning to think," as one student succinctly observed, "has many practical applications."

Finally, *private gain vs. public good:* Closely related to this question of whether the purpose of education is instrumental to career advancement or an end in itself is the ubiquitous question of whether the value of education (at a liberal arts college or elsewhere) is located in the private, personal development of the individual student or in public, social benefits, such as producing an educated workforce and an informed, engaged citizenry. Perhaps even more clearly than the other dualities we have explored, this one has always been profoundly conjoined (and indeed collapsed) by the purposes of a residential liberal arts education. There is far more to be said about this point, but for now I speak only from personal experience with undergraduates and alumni/ae of liberal arts colleges who are driven to academic success and seek its extension in good jobs and rich private lives, but who are at the same time committed to making and supporting difficult, responsible public choices. They serve their families and hometowns and they spread hope around the world; they create new businesses and serve great nonprofit causes. They do not think the world can be reduced to either/or's or that our most urgent problems can be solved if we see things too quickly as true or false, good or bad, or even mine or yours.

The tensions and contradictions held together by the liberal arts college model today are not always perfectly healthy and easily resolved. Challenges of fragmentation and incoherence accompany our innovation and evolution, and the balance between creative and dysfunctional tension is always hard to strike. For example, sometimes the dual demands of intense academic and extracurricular pursuits can stretch a student too far; and as in so many spheres, what is good for the individual is not always what is good for the group. At liberal arts colleges, and throughout life, we repeatedly struggle to give up one thing or the other and make hard choices among competing goods. Tolerating ambiguity cannot be allowed to mean easy moral relativism. But tensions and contradictions embraced as part of real, complicated life make people human and humane, just as they make institutions dynamic and proactive.

CHALLENGES FOR LIBERAL ARTS COLLEGES: RANKINGS, FACULTY, DIVERSITY

If the liberal arts college mission is as clear and effective and potentially "scalable" in some regards as I have suggested, what accounts for what I will call its marginalization in most discussions about American higher education today? There are several answers to that question, and the most common one is cost. Others have attempted to explain the complexity of liberal arts college pricing, but to a large extent their efforts fail to illuminate and change public understanding (or lack thereof). If we talk about costs at all, both the simple "facts" (i.e., the sticker price of elite colleges and universities) and the complex economic analysis required to understand them (ranging from discussions of financial aid practices like discounting and merit vs. need-based aid to considerations of "uncontrollables" like utilities, library materials, and health benefits for all employees) are so overwhelming that the conversation masks or ignores what I see as the underlying problem: the misalignment between the purposes of a liberal arts college and dominant cultural values. What I mean by "misalignment" becomes clearer if we consider just three particularly vexing and visible problems that affect other sectors as well: heightened competition within the sector, as highlighted by rankings; faculty status, governance, and service; and demographic diversity.

Rankings. Like their larger counterparts in private, public, and for-profit sectors, liberal arts colleges are, as Michael McPherson has observed, "prisoners of the competitive situation."[29] They are particularly, though by no means exclusively, slaves to rankings—something else from which we may seek to be liberated.[30] A great deal of controversy has been generated in the past few years by critiques of *U.S. News* and other college rankings, and I do not intend to revisit that territory for long here, except to note first that the very process of establishing rankings, given the diversity of educational institutions in this country, exacerbates and complicates the stratification between sectors by emphasizing (and in some sense manufacturing) competitive market forces within sectors. We do not know exactly how much rankings matter or to whom, but there is evidence that as they differentiate colleges and universities on various criteria, creating a hierarchy of schools within sectors, they are likely to be most meaningful for students with high incomes, advantages, and aspirations. As the recently discussed problem of "undermatching" further suggests, students from less privileged situations not only care less about rankings but may in fact be disadvantaged when schools work hard to improve their position through student selectivity measures.[31]

Rankings highlight another issue: It has been repeatedly suggested that if we do not like the existing media-driven rankings, we ought to be able to propose our own, more accurate and meaningful alternative, or that some noncommercial central authority should do it for us. But no one has yet produced a way of measuring "educational quality" accurately, and the more complex the purpose, the harder it should be to quantify results.[32] While the pressure to do more assessment has led to some interesting conversations and valuable practices on many campuses, the discourse and practice of assessment and accountability are at best immature. It remains difficult (and to the extent that it can be done, time-consuming and costly) to evaluate in complicated words, let alone simple numbers, what higher education at its best makes possible over the course of a single human life or throughout a complex culture; if it were easy to quantify holistic learning or transformative teaching or lifelong development, we would willingly do it. A study by the Institute for Higher Education Policy (IHEP) of international rankings reveals that this is a worldwide problem. There is no global consensus about how to assess and demonstrate educational quality, and so at present various nations and regions use widely divergent indicators, weightings, and methods.[33]

This level of uncertainty, however, can only feed the perception that we do not know or care enough about accountability or what our purposes really are. That perception masks the misalignment I mentioned above between what the general college-going population is looking for and what liberal arts colleges have to offer. External stakeholders prefer the simplicity and stability of rankings not only because Americans like to rank everything, but also because rankings appear to make costly and critical choices more informed by rendering an increasingly complex system and a bewildering sea of data and marketing "simple, fast, and easy," or at least somewhat more manageable and comprehensible. External stakeholders also want something they perceive as "unbiased," and it is easy to understand why much of our heartfelt reporting on the value of higher education could be perceived as promotional hype. Whenever we speak, as we must, about the lofty aims, the long-term, intangible value and values of a liberal arts college, we risk being heard as PR agents rather than as educators.

It may be that the rankings, like big-time sports, present a problem we ought to leave alone because it cannot be alleviated and distracts us from more important work.[34] I can offer no easy suggestions for the collaborative problem-solving needed in this arena. The best discussions I have seen come from policy institutes like IHEP, which are independent of one sector or another. I would also note that on this issue, institutions of higher education—from community colleges to research universities—may still have far more in common with one another than with the for-profit media or government. Although finding the resources to support such projects will be increasingly difficult, we could individually or in consortia sponsor and then discuss more and better research into the influence of rankings, here and around the world. Anticipating an argument I'll make later, I might add that thinking more broadly as educators, we could also call for and support studies that would help us see, theorize, and better manage for strategic purposes the conflicting and at present irreconcilable values within American higher education—between, say, meritocracy and inclusiveness or excellence and equity, or between education as a social/public good (demanding transparency and collaboration) and an individual/private benefit (which inevitably entails competition).

The professoriate. A second critical fault-line in the liberal arts college model centers on issues of faculty status, leadership, service, and governance. Most small liberal arts colleges still offer tenure-track (or comparable) positions to the majority of their faculty members. But it is not clear that we benefit adequately from what that should mean for the way our institutions or higher education in general work. At a time when we need to collaborate internally and externally to be resilient, creative, and flexible, the polarization of administration and faculty seems only to be growing. From the faculty perspective, the administration even at a small college is perceived to be increasingly corporate, excessively large, transient, focused on the financial bottom line, overly ambitious, and inadequately respectful and consultative of faculty culture. From the administrators' point of view, faculty members may seem to have their heads in the sand; they don't pay attention to the facts or attempt to think strategically or institutionally, and instead they may use the chief weapon in their arsenal, the power to resist change, to block simultaneously both the belt-tightening that administrators are forced to lead and the innovation that they would like to lead. Moreover, as an offshoot of stratification between sectors, under most circumstances there is little interaction or common ground between the tenured or tenure-track professor at "Lawn and Library College" who teaches four courses a year with a sabbatical every seventh semester to sustain a brilliant resume, and the adjunct professor teaching 12 courses a year at various "Commuter U's" and "Computer U's."

As we imagine young Ph.D. candidates facing these utterly divided and incommensurate career paths, higher education leaders must worry about where we will find talented teachers and researchers in the future. The degree of misalignment we see between academe and public opinion is in this instance exacerbated by the largely cost-driven misalignment within the educational community. The professoriate is in a certain disarray, not only divided from potential allies and partners in other, related professional groups but separated within its own ranks. While institutions face widely different challenges in this regard, we could benefit from working together to develop more strategies and seize more opportunities to build bridges between administrators and faculty within institutions, and between faculty members in different kinds of positions across institutions and sectors.[35]

Diversity. Diversity is both an advantage and a third potential source of incoherence and vulnerability for liberal arts colleges, and a complex consideration for higher education today that I can mention only briefly here. Social justice and access for students from underrepresented groups are important priorities for liberal arts colleges, many of which have outperformed larger universities in realizing the benefits of diversifying their campuses. On this issue, liberal arts colleges may also be somewhat more well aligned with general culture and the marketplace (where, for instance, diversity has become an important part of corporate strategy). It is frequently observed, however, that anticipated demographic shifts may weaken if not destroy many liberal arts colleges, most of which are located in areas of the country where population growth in the groups from whom they traditionally recruit is declining, and few of which are at present intrinsically attractive to or designed for the majority of high school graduates.

Confronting this challenge, we might have something useful to learn and gain from working with bigger institutions. For instance, although only a few extended examples of this strategy can be found, it seems worth thinking about how more small liberal arts colleges could form mutually beneficial partnerships with larger urban institutions and community colleges to improve access, climate, and reach. One contribution liberal arts colleges might in turn bring to such partnerships is their capacity and desire as small-scale communities to seek and refine intentional strategies for realizing in practice the theoretical and rhetorical benefits of diversity broadly defined. In a recent national faculty survey in which the majority of the faculty at Bates College participated, one principle generated the greatest consensus: a diverse student body enhances the experience of all students. On that same survey, 100 percent of our faculty who responded said the most important goal of the college was to develop the ability to think critically. Taken together, results like this converge on the principle I discussed earlier: the integral connection between diversity and the development of a robust and variegated intellectual toolkit for all students.

If college is to be in some sense "for all," we need to develop a national agenda for higher education that does not blur key distinctions but does address concerns that may be relevant across sectors, and virtually all institutions of higher education today face the challenges I have named—the problems of competition, faculty, and diversity. Common problems create allies, and if we can identify and focus on issues like these that cut across the growing gaps between sectors, we may be able to boost our ability to take collective action, joining forces to influence and improve policy and practice. Liberal arts colleges may provide a particularly good place to begin experimenting with solutions to some of these problems not only because they are smaller and potentially more manageable institutions, but also because they are quite demonstrably long-lived and resilient ones.

*   *   *

The durability and efficacy of the liberal arts college model derives from the strong practices and principles I have outlined here—calling students to what is complex, difficult, and slow; cultivating focus and participation; offering some degree of "time out" and immunity from immediate consequences; sustaining friendship and learning in community; embracing contradictions. These practices, which are needed now more than ever, serve to shape what I have called the liberated consumer by giving each student not only the capacity for individual agency but also a sense of responsibility and commitment to collective well-being. President Obama's insistence that quitting high school is "quitting on your country" implicitly acknowledges the dangers of unfettered consumerism and "being uniquely, completely, imperially alone." Liberal arts colleges today educate liberated, conscious, citizen-consumers using a distinctive recipe that generally calls for 4 years in residence, low student-faculty ratios, abundant options for cocurricular and extracurricular activities, a broadly diverse yet commonly motivated student body, and other increasingly rare (and expensive) ingredients. But if the core purposes and principles were seen as important, there could be other ways to approach them. Whatever the curriculum, it could be explicitly framed by similar objectives for all students: to embrace an appropriate level of challenge, pay attention, seek and be granted time for reflection, prize participation, and offer friendship. Some goals might be even more easily achieved in "vocational training"—such as the notion of production and participation, which is understood as an antidote to passive consumption.

To say that we have *some* fundamental purposes in common, furthermore, is not to say we have *all* purposes in common, or that all institutions of higher education need to be designed to do the same thing at the same time in the same way. Just like the purposes of liberal arts colleges, the purposes of the entire American system of higher education or further education—running the gamut from 1-year training programs to research universities—could be seen as appropriately multiple and diverse and sometimes, indeed, contradictory. The contradictions and tensions between sectors will block any movement at all if we are trying to reduce the purposes of education to some unitary, easily measured goals—or if we overindulge in market competition. But if we also acknowledge here that in fact its contradictions and tensions are at the very heart of what makes American higher education a highly complicated, interesting, and creative system for educating liberated consumers, the next big question becomes clear: Where and how can we acknowledge, understand, celebrate, and then leverage our multiple, complicated purposes more effectively?

NOTES

1. This part of the president's speech reads as follows: "It is our responsibility as lawmakers and educators to make this system work. But it is the responsibility of every citizen to participate in it. And so tonight, I ask every American to commit to at least one year or more of higher education or career training. This can be community college or a four-year school; vocational training or an apprenticeship. But whatever the training may be, every American will need to get more than a high school diploma. And dropping out of high school is no longer an option. It's not just quitting

on yourself, it's quitting on your country—and this country needs and values the talents of every American. That is why we will provide the support necessary for you to complete college and meet a new goal: by 2020, America will once again have the highest proportion of college graduates in the world." "Remarks of President Barack Obama," Address to Joint Session of Congress, February 24, 2009.

2. Patricia Albjerg Graham, "Schools: Cacophony about Practice, Silence about Purpose," *Daedalus*, 113, no. 4 (Fall 1984), 55.

3. In a personal communication, Bryk laments this absence of a common understanding of the purposes of education today and suggests that without attention to this problem, we will never develop "a shared, energetic resolve to make change." Even in the most affluent neighborhoods of Silicon Valley, moreover, Bryk notes that he found exquisite taste in wine, food, cars, and homes existing side by side with astounding ignorance about what excellence in education would look like, and tolerance of educational institutions and experiences that are at best mediocre.

4. Francis Oakley, ed., "Introduction," *Liberal Arts Colleges in American Higher Education* (New York: ACLS, 2005); for a recent articulation of this position, see Roger G. Baldwin and Vicki L. Baker, "The Case of the Disappearing Liberal Arts College," *Inside Higher Education*, http://www.insidehighered.com/views/2009/07/09/baldwin

5. See, for example, David D. Dill, "The Public Good, the Public Interest, and Public Higher Education": "The growing rivalry among institutions of higher education has become a contest for academic prestige, not a competition for the most effective production of human capital." Dill cites research suggesting that investing in "student consumption benefits" is a way of drawing high ability students rather than "improving educational quality," http://www.unc.edu/ppaq/docs/PublicvsPrivate.pdf

6. Kim Benston, "Beyond the Circle: Challenges and Opportunities for the Contemporary Liberal Arts Teacher-Scholar," in Oakley, ed., *Liberal Arts Colleges*, 98, emphasis added.

7. For a recent discussion of the confusion about liberal arts and liberal education, see Maurice O'Sullivan, "Artes Illiberales: The Four Myths of Liberal Education," *Change*, 41, no. 5 (September/October 2009): 20–27.

8. Alexander W. Astin and Mitchell J. Chang, "Colleges That Emphasize Research and Teaching: Can You Have Your Cake and Eat It Too?" *Change*, 27, no. 5 (September/October 1995): 44–49.

9. For a compelling recent argument about why students today choose liberal arts colleges, see Mary Marcy, "Alive and Well," *Inside Higher Education*, December 28, 2009, http://www.insidehighered.com/views/2009/12/28/marcy

10. For the phrase see Benston, "Beyond the Circle."

11. Benjamin Barber, *Consumed: How Markets Corrupt Children, Infantilize Adults, and Swallow Citizens Whole* (New York: W. W. Norton, 2007), 126.

12. Matt Miller, *The Tyranny of Dead Ideas: Letting Go of the Old Ways of Thinking to Unleash a New Prosperity* (New York: Times Books, 2009), 31.

13. Barber, *Consumed*, 14.

14. Ibid., 127.

15. See Ibid., chap. 3, for a discussion of the process of maturation "in which the move from (say) easy to hard or simple to complex or fast to slow takes the form of an evolution in which something of the child (the easy, the simple, and the fast) is retained and elaborated in the fully evolved adults" (pp. 83–84).

16. Alfred North Whitehead, "Universities and Their Function," *The Aims of Education* (New York: Free Press, 1957), 93.

17. David Brooks, "Lost in the Crowd," *New York Times*, December 15, 2008, http://www.nytimes.com/2008/12/16/opinion/16brooks.html

18. "David Foster Wallace on Life and Work," adapted from a commencement speech given to the 2005 graduating class at Kenyon College, http://online.wsj.com/article/SB122178211966454607.html

19. Johan Huizinga, *Homo Ludens: A Study of the Play Element in Culture* (Boston: Beacon Press, 1955).

20. Bill Gaver, "Designing for Homo Ludens," *I3 Magazine*, no. 12 (June 2002): 2.

21. "David Foster Wallace on Life and Work."

22. Peter Elbow, *Writing Without Teachers* (New York: Oxford University Press, 1998), 76. This work continues to be an influential text a generation after its initial publication in 1973. In 1998, *Writing Without Teachers* was republished on the 25th anniversary of its debut. Quotations are taken from this edition.

23. Ibid., 148.

24. Ibid., xxii–xxiii.

25. Ibid., 148.

26. Ibid., xxiv.

27. Ibid., xxii.

28. "Without other people to work with," Elbow writes, "we have no strong tool for coming up with competing ideas—which is our leverage for testing. And we have no strong tool for entering into alien or foreign ideas except by having fans of those ideas tell us about them and describe the view from inside them . . . . We can get along without teachers, but only if we make primary use of a group of people sharing their experiences with each other—using a process that invites the maximum multiplicity or divergence of views and asks participants not to quarrel with what looks odd or alien but to try to experience and enter into it." Ibid., xxv, emphasis added.

29. Response to Lapovsky and Kaufman in Oakley, ed., *Liberal Arts Colleges in American Higher Education*, p. 82 ("commodity-like marketing presentation and comparison of educational services through rankings and lists in combination with an increasing consumer mentality focusing on convenience, service, quality and cost"). Both domains (classroom and civic square) "equally face the threat not only of being saturated, indeed engulfed, by market forces . . . ." (Benston, 101).

30. See David D. Dill, "Will Market Competition Assure Academic Quality? An Analysis of the UK and US Experience," in *Quality Assurance in Higher Education: Trends in Regulation, Translation and Transformation*, ed. Westerheijden et al. (Dordrecht,

The Netherlands: Springer, 2007), 47–72, for a comparative study of the relationship between competition and quality.

31. See Dill, "The Public Good," and "Will Market Competition Assure Academic Quality?," 63, and "Impact of College Rankings on Institutional Decision Making: Four Country Case Studies," *IHEP Issue Brief* (May 2009): 8.

32. See, for example, "Engaged or Confused?" *Inside Higher Education* (November 9, 2009), http://www.insidehighered.com/news/2009/11/09/porter

33. "College and University Ranking Systems: Global Perspectives and American Challenges," *IHEP Issue Brief* (April 2007): 23.

34. Zemsky, "The Don'ts of Higher Education Reform," *Inside Higher Education* (September 4, 2009), http://www.insidehighered.com/views/2009/09/04/zemsky

35. For one recent discussion of the problem of engaging the professoriate in "institutional thinking," however, see Louis Menand, "Interdisciplinarity and Anxiety," http://humanities.princeton.edu/fds/MenandInterdisciplinarity.pdf. Menand points to a particularly difficult dimension of the problem when he observes, "There is one more move in the evolution of the modern profession. This is when the institutional piece drops out of the formal picture. This is what Stanley Fish, who has written a lot of interesting things about professionalism in the academy, calls the anti-professionalism that is a requisite part of being an academic professional. I think this is a pretty accurate observation about the relation most academics have to the institutional and organizational apparatus that credentializes and supports them."

CHAPTER 4

The Other 75%:
College Education Beyond the Elite

Paul Attewell
David E. Lavin

Decades ago, the cover of the *New Yorker* magazine reproduced a color cartoon by Saul Steinberg representing a view of the United States as seen from Manhattan. Three quarters of the picture was reserved for the avenues on Manhattan's West Side. The distant parts of the country were mainly left bare, but the word "Chicago" appeared somewhere near Canada on the right and a small bump appeared in the distance, labeled "The Rockies." At the very top, a smidgen of the canvas was allotted for the Pacific Ocean with Asia peeking over the horizon.

Steinberg's cartoon poked fun at the parochialism of Manhattanites, who view their own neighborhood as the center of the world. Unfortunately, a similar parochialism affects views of higher education in America. There are close to 17 million undergraduates seeking degrees in the United States. Their numbers are booming: enrollments increased by 24% between 2000 and 2008, and are expected to climb to 19 million by 2019.[1] However, as we document below, only a small minority of these 17 million college students fit the popular stereotype of a full-time student living in a dorm on a college campus, financially supported by her or his parents. Nevertheless, public discussion and current government policies predominantly reflect the concerns of this stereotypical kind of student, despite their being numerically unrepresentative.

We need to move beyond a Steinberg cartoon of academe and carefully consider the system of mass higher education that has emerged in America over the last half century. Most of today's undergraduates are not in the same situation as their counterparts were 40 years ago, and serious discussions about the purposes of education, about pedagogy and curriculum, as well as government policies toward higher education, need to be rooted in an accurate understanding of who today's students are. Attending to the larger picture, rather than the atypical situation of the elite, affords insights into debates over degree completion and time to degree; about affirmative action and social justice; issues of access and affordability; and about the role of a liberal arts education versus vocational education.

In this chapter, we focus on four topics, beginning with a demographic portrait of today's undergraduates and documenting how dramatically the typical student career has changed in recent decades. We then make some points about students' choices of major and the economic payoff to various kinds of higher education. Third, we touch upon access to higher education and the current funding climate. Given this context, we turn to the fourth topic: the issues of purpose and pedagogy in higher education that the other contributors to this volume have already highlighted, with the proviso that we are concerned about these matters particularly as they apply to the mass of undergraduates today, as distinct from those students who attend elite colleges.

WHO ARE TODAY'S UNDERGRADUATES?

For many, the word "undergraduate" brings to mind a young person, fresh out of high school, a full-time student who is financially dependent on his or her parents. Statisticians refer to this type as the "traditional undergraduate." Numerically speaking, this image of a college student is quite out of date. Defined in the government statisticians' way, traditional undergraduates had become a numerical minority in American academia by the late 1970s. By 1990, only a third of undergraduates fully fit the traditional pattern. By the year 2000, fewer than one quarter of undergraduates were fully traditional, and that proportion continues to shrink.[2]

The "traditional" category shrinks even below one quarter if commuter students are excluded from that category. Fewer than 14% of America's undergraduates live on campus: the bulk of today's college students commute. Many of them would love to live in a dorm and go to a "real college" but that is beyond their financial reach. Tuition plus room and board at residential public 4-year colleges averages $16,140 per year; the equivalent figure at private 4-year colleges is $36,993.[3] Commuting is often dictated by family finances: the least painful way that parents can help their offspring is by providing room and board at home and having their child attend a local college.

The most important divergence between the bulk of today's undergraduates and the "traditional" student profile is that the large majority of today's undergraduates combine college with paid work: 82% of undergraduates nationwide say they can't afford to go to school without working.[4] Over a third of undergraduates are employed full-time while enrolled, and 44% more work part-time during term time. College life is very different for undergraduates who work for all or part of their living or for educational expenses, compared to traditional students who are fully supported by parents combined with financial aid.

Federal financial aid policies reflect an earlier era when most undergraduates came from relatively affluent families and were financially dependent on their parents. Those policies are disadvantageous for working undergraduates, compared to students who do not work, and are toughest of all for young students who are financially self-supporting.

Legislators were worried that affluent parents might evade their responsibilities by declaring their offspring independent, so they enacted regulations that automatically classified almost all undergraduates under the age of 24 as financial dependants of their parents, for purposes of calculating need and federal aid.[5] Sociologically speaking, this policy is nonsense. Low-income and working-class undergraduates who are 18 or older are often de facto independent. In many cases, their parents cannot afford to support them and put them through college, so students try to support themselves. This is often a matter of cultural expectations: less affluent parents typically expect their college-age offspring to shoulder some if not all of the financial burden of higher education. Moreover, undergraduates age 18 and older frequently share this view: they think of themselves as adults and agree they should be largely self-sufficient. The result is that about three quarters of today's undergraduates work for pay while in school, and many of them are trying to complete a degree while earning a substantial proportion of their living and educational costs.

The working undergraduate phenomenon is widespread even among students from more affluent families. About one in five American teenagers works part-time during high school to pay for their clothes, for gas money, and for leisure.[6] This is looked upon positively by some middle-class parents as well as by parents from financially stressed families. A part-time job is a sign of a youth's responsibility and self-reliance, and an opportunity to develop good work habits. By the time teenagers leave high school for college, many feel an acute need to assert their adulthood and sense of responsibility by working. At a minimum—even if their parents foot most of the college bill—many students plan to earn the $300 to $1,000 dollars a month that the typical undergraduate spends on food, dating, and leisure.[7]

Everywhere except for the richest private colleges, financial aid does not come close to covering the full costs of living and attending college: there is an unfunded gap. The federal formula, on which colleges' financial aid decisions are made, typically assumes that parents will provide a substantial monetary contribution to fill this gap, known as the "Expected Family Contribution," or EFC. But substantial numbers of parents are not making this contribution, and the result is that many of America's undergraduates are working while enrolled, some out of necessity–because their parents can't or won't pay–and some out of choice, because the student feels parents shouldn't have to pay the full EFC. These students are working during term time to fill the gap between their expenses and the financial aid they receive, without the Expected Family Contribution.

For the stereotypical traditional student, college is a protected interlude between high school and adulthood, a time-out before life in the real world begins. By contrast, for the nontraditional undergraduates who predominate today, college life is no time-out but rather an obstacle race of economic stress and cross pressures between family, work, and education. The "real world" has forced its way into collegiate lives, and the undergraduate years have become blended into adult life. This is most frequently the case for working-class students attending nonselective commuter universities, but the same cultural patterns affect some students at the flagship public universities, and even a few less affluent students in elite private colleges.

The competing demands of paid work and school faced by so many of today's undergraduates profoundly affect students' level of academic engagement, in terms of how much time they spend reading and studying, their participation in campus life, and their choices of major. Perhaps most importantly, these demands have transformed the length and structure of undergraduate careers.

First, about one third of undergraduates now delay college for a year or more after graduating from high school.[8] These delayed entrants come disproportionately from lower-income and minority families. Some may be unsure of whether they want to go to college; others need to earn some money before they can afford to begin their studies. Irrespective of motivation, delayed entry is associated with markedly worse odds of completing a degree.

A second response to the high cost of college attendance and the need to work to finance one's studies is to start one's undergraduate career at a 2-year or community college rather than at a 4-year institution. Average tuition plus fees at a public 2-year college was $2,713 in 2009–2010, compared to $7,605 at a public 4-year college–a considerable savings.[9] Consequently, enrollments at 2-year colleges have been booming, and currently about 48% of enrollment in public colleges is in 2-year institutions.[10]

About one quarter of the degree students who start their college careers at 2-year colleges aspire to a 4-year degree. Their hope is that they can accumulate many of their credits in the cheaper kind of institution and then transfer to a 4-year college to complete their BA. In theory this is a cost-effective strategy. In practice, many who take this route slow down or fall by the wayside: only half of those who start at a community college aiming at a bachelor's degree successfully transfer, and fewer than half of those transfers have made it to the BA within 6 years.[11]

A third response to rising costs by many of today's undergraduates is to cycle in and out of college over time, often to earn money for rent, tuition, or fees for the following semester or to cope with family needs. Among degree students entering 2-year colleges, 81% stop out at some point, and 56% of those who do ultimately complete an AA or BA degree have stopped out for a semester or more. For degree students entering 4-year colleges, 34% stop out for one semester or more.[12] Stopping out is deleterious for one's chances of graduating in both kinds of institutions, but is associated with much worse outcomes in 4-year colleges.

Some students avoid stopping out, but instead reduce their course load to part-time when employment or other demands become too pressing. Part-time enrollment is also cheaper, because then tuition is lower. Fewer than half of today's undergraduates are exclusively full-time enrollees, sometimes because they are unable to earn enough to support themselves and simultaneously take a full course load. Part-time attendance is a compromise.

In concert, these forces have lengthened the typical time to a bachelor's degree well beyond 4 years. A study of a nationally representative sample of bachelor's degree recipients found that only 39% of these graduates finished their degree within 4 years of entering college. Another 48% took between 4 and 10 years to graduate and 14% of the graduates took over 10 years from college entry to their BA.[13] These figures are averaged across all types of institutions and kinds of students. If one looks at subpopulations, the picture grows more extreme: time to degree is considerably longer for minorities and for less affluent students in general.

Another consequence of the cycling in and out pattern is that nearly 60% of students nowadays earn their BA from a different institution than the one they first entered. Even among the most privileged stratum—BAs who begin at private doctoral-granting universities—over 40% change university before graduating.

Patterns of cycling in and out of college, of attending part-time, and of transferring from one college to another are largely driven by students' financial, work, and family circumstances. Yet policy makers clamor to treat graduation rates as performance measures that indicate whether a particular college is doing its job well or badly. There have been repeated attempts at both the federal and state levels to reward those colleges with high graduation rates and penalize institutions with low graduate rates, alongside efforts to codify and publicize these measures of college performance.

Policy makers act as if the cycling and transfer patterns were aberrant and avoidable, and under the control of colleges, rather than the new norm. To the extent that federal and state policies reward shorter time-to-degree or emphasize higher institutional graduation rates, they benefit colleges that serve more affluent students: undergraduates who can afford to attend full time, and who don't stop out to work. To the extent that policies penalize colleges with a longer time-to-degree or lower graduation rates, they punish institutions that disproportionately serve less affluent and minority students.

Ongoing efforts by policy makers to hold universities "accountable" for average time-to-degree and graduation rates are therefore creating powerful incentives for colleges to "move upmarket," since time-to-degree and graduation numbers will certainly improve if a college enrolls more affluent or fewer low-income students, or avoids working and part-time students. While there are undoubtedly some initiatives that university administrators can take to improve graduation rates and time-to-degree, even with their current kinds of students, enrolling more affluent students and/or avoiding the most economically and academically stressed students will provide quick and reliable improvements on these outcomes. In other words, recent policy initiatives are unwittingly creating perverse incentives that contradict the goals of access and inclusion.

COLLEGE MAJORS

Some commentators are distressed by curriculum changes that have taken place in higher education over the last half century. One recurrent concern is that the liberal arts majors, a signature feature of American colleges, are in decline or under threat because of a rise in the popularity of vocational majors (see Table 4.1).

What are the implications of mass higher education for the liberal arts as a course of study? Nationwide, across a representative sample of BA recipients in 1993, about one third majored in so-called academic subjects, while roughly two thirds majored in career-oriented subjects, of which business and education were the most numerous.[14] However, this one third figure taking "academic majors" gives an inflated impression, because this category includes majors like economics and biology that are filled with career-oriented students on business and medical school tracks.

A more informative statistic is that, nationally, just under 10% of BAs majored in arts and humanities and another 3% in the physical sciences and mathematics. More recent data, for BA graduates in 2007–2008, use a different taxonomy of majors but paint a similar picture, with about 13% of bachelor's degrees conferred in the arts and humanities and 1.4% in the physical sciences.[15] These numbers on majors seem to validate the worry that the liberal arts are in decline.

One might jump to the conclusion that students at non-selective colleges are opting for career-oriented majors, while undergraduates at highly selective colleges retain a commitment to the arts and humanities. But that is not what American academe looks like today! Instead we find that

Table 4.1. Percentage Distribution of 1992–1993 Bachelor's Degree Recipients' Undergraduate Major

Undergraduate major	Total	Male	Female
Total	100.0	100.0	100.0
Academic:	**34.6**	**34.0**	**35.1**
Social and behavioral sciences	13.1	12.5	13.5
Arts and humanities	9.9	9.1	10.6
Biological Sciences	4.4	5.3	3.7
Mathematics & physical sciences	3.2	4.0	2.5
Other academic	4.1	3.2	4.7
Career-oriented:	**65.4**	**66.0**	**65.0**
Business & management	23.0	27.0	19.7
Education	13.0	5.9	18.8
Health	6.8	3.4	9.6
Engineering	6.4	12.1	1.8
Computer Science	2.2	3.3	1.3
Other career-oriented	14.0	14.3	13.8

Source: Susan Choy and C. Dennis Carroll, *Ten Years After College* (Washington, D.C.: National Center for Education Statistics, U.S. Dept. of Education, 2008), 55; also Baccalaureate and Beyond Study Longitudinal Study (B&B 93/03).

undergraduates across the social class and institutional spectrum view college as a crucial step toward finding a well-paying job, and that the large majority of students pick majors with careers in mind.

The likelihood of taking a so-called academic major is only weakly associated with institutional selectivity. Career-oriented majors are very common everywhere. Private doctoral universities have only a slightly higher percentage of their students enrolled in academic majors than other kinds of colleges. Even among private liberal arts colleges there is no strong preference toward academic majors. (Liberal arts colleges produced 17.7% of the nation's BAs overall, 17.7% of academic major BAs, and 19.8% of arts and humanities BAs.) It is not the case, therefore, that selective private colleges preserve the liberal arts, while vocational education dominates elsewhere.

Family background *is* related to college major. Students whose parents went no further than high school are skewed toward career—rather than academic majors. At the other extreme, undergraduates whose parents have advanced degrees constitute one quarter of the survey sample, but account for 36% of arts and humanities BAs.

These numbers do not imply, however, that students from more affluent or more highly educated families are any less career-oriented than other
students. Instead, it seems likely that students from highly educated families
who declare undergraduate majors in the arts and humanities may be willing to do so because these majors remain stepping stones to law or other
professional schools. If one grants this assumption, then it becomes evident
that almost *all* American undergraduates are to a considerable extent career-
oriented in their choice of major, and that undergraduate majors in the humanities and arts survive largely because they are established feeders into
professional schools.

The implication we draw from this in terms of curriculum and pedagogy
is that it makes little sense to decry current undergraduates' choice of majors
or deplore the emphasis placed on the economic value of degrees. If the liberal arts are to flourish, they will have to do so intertwined with the heavily
vocational orientation that dominates American undergraduate life, largely
as ingredients of, rather than alternatives to, the educational experiences of
undergraduates pursuing career-relevant majors.

THE PAYOFF TO A DEGREE AND TO SPECIFIC MAJORS

Despite the huge expansion of American higher education over the last
half century, the value of a BA has not declined. On the contrary, the
earnings gap between high school graduates and bachelor's degree holders
has grown over time and now averages almost $22,000 per year.[16] A large
payoff is evident for all racial and ethnic groups and across social classes.[17]
Moreover, academically weak high school students who enter college gain
a clear earnings boost, not just high-performing students. Even if a student
does *not* complete a college degree, the financial rewards for attending college are substantial: on average workers with incomplete college earn 17%
more than their counterparts who are high school graduates.[18] Given these
earnings differences, one would expect student demand for college access
to remain high. Indeed, current government projections suggest a 12% increase in undergraduate enrollment between 2006 and 2017.[19]

In purely monetary terms, however, arts and humanities majors are a
worse choice than career-oriented ones. The national *Baccalaureate and Beyond* survey followed students for 10 years after their BA graduation in 1993
until 2003. By that time, the average student with a career major earned
considerably more than an arts and humanities major. Table 4.2 contains
some examples.

These figures almost certainly understate the earnings penalty associated
with academic degree majors, because many of the students who majored in

Table 4.2. Average Earnings for Full-time Employees in 2003 by Bachelor Degree Major

Social & Behavioral Sciences	$62,300
Arts & Humanities	$52,800
Biological Sciences	$62,200
Math & Physical Sciences	$58,200
Business & Management	$65,900
Education	$43,800
Health	$65,000
Engineering	$74,900
Computer Science	$72,600

Source: Susan Choy and C. Dennis Carroll, *Ten Years After College* (Washington, D.C.: National Center for Education Statistics, U.S. Dept. of Education, 2008), 55; also Baccalaureate and Beyond Study Longitudinal Study (B&B 93/03).

academic subjects have gone beyond their BAs to obtain professional and higher degrees. Some undoubtedly transformed themselves into highly paid lawyers or business professionals. Despite the fact that incomes of people with these advanced law and business degrees are classified under the person's undergraduate major in the table above, on average arts and humanities majors experience an enduring earnings handicap, exceeded in size only by that for education majors.

Undergraduates are not purely profit-maximizing creatures; some follow an intellectual agenda irrespective of its monetary reward, and others are poorly informed about their ultimate earnings prospects. To the extent that students do respond to material incentives, however, they are going to be drawn away from the arts and humanities and away from "academic majors."

ACCESS AND EQUITY

Changes in the undergraduate student body have evolved over a long time period. The expansion of higher education in America in the last half century has been tremendous. Enrollments grew more than eightfold, from just above 2 million in 1950 to nearly 17 million today. All groups have benefited from this expansion. As Table 4.3 indicates, overall college-going among high school graduates increased from around 50% in 1972 to over 80% in 1992.

Enrollments have grown substantially among ethnic minorities, women, and low-income students. College enrollments have also swelled among academically weaker students: individuals with high school averages of C or below (and among these, substantial percentages were accepted into 4-year colleges). Overall, the new recruits to higher education represent a cutting edge—over half are the first generation in their families to attend college. And among minority students, between two thirds and three quarters are the first generation.

But despite the expansion among all groups, inequalities in college enrollment remain: Whites are still more likely to enroll than minorities, and high-income students remain much more likely to enroll than lower-income students. Among affluent and academically strong students, college enrollment has become almost universal.

Table 4.3. Trends in College Attendance Among High School Graduates by Cohort

Percentage of all High school graduates	1972	1982	1992
	53	66	81
Race			
White	54	69	83
Black	51	57	70
Hispanic	39	54	79
Gender			
Male	53	63	80
Female	54	69	83
SES			
Top Quintile	79	88	98
Second Quintile	62	78	90
Third quintile	50	61	81
Fourth quintile	41	50	65
Bottom quintile	33	37	58
High School Grades			
A	82	94	97
B	64	82	89
C	41	66	77
C- or below	23	45	59

Source: Paul Attewell and David E. Lavin, *Passing the Torch: Does Higher Education for the Disadvantaged Pay Off Across the Generations?* (New York: Russell Sage, 2007).

Although there has been great controversy about inequalities and affirmative action in elite colleges, there has, at the same time, been a backlash against expansion in those colleges that are unselective. Unselective colleges encompass around 75% of enrollments.

The critics say that:

1. Too many students are not "college material."
2. Weaker students have scandalously low graduation rates.
3. Because of downgrading that has occurred among students, college degrees are not worth much anymore.

These criticisms provide part of the context for a book we wrote, so we will summarize some of our conclusions here, and point readers who desire more evidence to the book itself.[20]

Most of the "scandal" of low graduation rates comes from applying to the new students, who now predominate, a conception of college careers based on the period when traditional students dominated enrollments. To show the miscalculation this can produce, if we take the 17-college City University of New York (CUNY) system, where there exists 30 years of data, and use the most commonly cited figure that measures graduation within a 6-year time frame, we would erroneously classify as "dropouts" 25% of White women who eventually graduated. We'd also measure as dropouts 56% of Black women whom our longer data indicate did complete a degree, plus 53% of Hispanic women.

This is not just a methodological issue. Intervals such as 6 years, which form the bedrock for government reports and policy about degree completion, overstate ethnic differences in graduation rates and therefore add to the impression of minority students as high-risk students. Longer periods of time to measure graduation rates reveal ethnic differences to be narrower.

Another aspect of graduation concerns postgraduate work. More than a third of those who completed bachelor's degrees at CUNY went on to complete a postgraduate degree (an MA, Ph.D., or advanced degree), so expanded access has paid off even at the top levels of the higher education system.

Despite delayed graduation, college continues to make a big economic difference in the lives of students. Large increases in access have not undercut the value of educational credentials. Table 4.4 shows that higher levels of educational attainment are clearly connected with increases in income. Although it is not shown in the table, we also know that payoffs now are higher than they used to be decades earlier. So, under a much more accessible system of mass higher education, college continues to pay off. Further, while we know that students who entered college with weak high school records did not earn as much as straight-A students, they nevertheless earned

Table 4.4. Mean Income by Educational Attainment for Male and Female Full-Time Year-Round Workers, 2008

Education Level	Men	Women
High School Graduates	$43,493	$31,666
Some College, no degree	$50,433	$36,019
Associate's degree	$54,830	$39,935
Bachelor's degree	$81,975	$54,207

Source: U.S. Census, www.census.gov/compendia/statab/2011/tables/11s0702.xls

significantly more annually than students from similar backgrounds who went no further than high school graduation.

FUNDING AND POLICY DIRECTIONS

These and related data imply that mass higher education has been very successful, if we measure success in terms of individual mobility and earnings. (We shall turn to more expansive definitions of educational purpose shortly.) Nevertheless, the public policy pendulum has been moving in an opposite direction in terms of access and academic progress. Some of the changes have been curricular. For example, there has been a national trend to end admission to 4-year colleges among students who are considered in need of remedial work.

In terms of fiscal policy and financial aid, recent developments have made access more difficult. As a proportion of state expenditures, appropriations for higher education have spiraled downward, so that by 2005, the investment effort of the states was only 65% of what it was in 1976. By 2005–2006 state appropriations amounted to only 27% of total revenues of public higher education institutions nationwide.[21] State appropriations per student were 19% lower in 2009–2010 on average than they'd been one decade earlier.[22] In some states, public colleges and universities now receive less than 10% of their revenue from state appropriations, rendering the label "state university" quite misleading.

Partly to offset the loss of revenue from state appropriations, tuition at public colleges has skyrocketed. This has coincided with a movement of federal and state aid away from need-based grants, a trend of special consequence for low-income students. In 1976 the main need-based aid, Pell grants, covered about 72% of costs at the average public 4-year school. By 2003 these grants covered only 38% of the cost. Financial aid has increasingly become "merit-based"–that is, dependent upon how well a student performed during high school. Since there is a positive association between high school grades and family income, merit aid ends up being disproportionately allocated to middle- and upper-income families.

In addition, tax policy has become an important financial aid vehicle. Tax credits allow taxpayers to deduct a share of tuition costs from federal taxes. Such credits mostly benefit middle and upper middle-income families.[23] However, under the current financial aid structure, low-income families have the largest need not covered by financial aid.

Proportionally fewer students from low-income and minority families are likely to enter college as a consequence of these trends in financial aid and tuition. But inadequate funding has more complex results than just preventing enrollment. Students with unmet financial need may delay matriculation immediately after high school, or may choose less expensive shorter-term programs, such as 2-year community colleges or technical programs in proprietary schools.[24] They may attend college part-time or interrupt their attendance by temporarily dropping out to save money. Such choices undoubtedly extend time to graduation and likely diminish the level of credential eventually attained.

What all of this adds up to is that there can be no complacency about the future of broad access. If broad access were to be rolled back, the consequences would be dramatic. Analyses in our book show that if access were reduced to where it was 30 or 40 years ago, it would diminish the proportion of people earning bachelor's degrees and it would especially reduce the proportion of minority students completing them. In the case of Blacks, for example, it would lower the proportion of BA degrees by about half. Overall, because of open access, the national sample we studied earned 41 billion dollars more in the year 2000 than it would have earned if broad access were rolled back.

The current economic crisis has led state governments to cut millions from their higher education budgets, making entry to college and completion more difficult.[25] In today's turbulent economic and political environment it is hard to see how matters are going to improve for "the other 75%."

THE PURPOSES OF MASS HIGHER EDUCATION

Much of the soul-searching about the erosion of liberal arts education and increasing vocationalism on campus has ignored the kinds of students enrolled in our system of mass higher education. It is a discourse written largely by academics in, or by graduates of, elite colleges. For example, Charles Murray, a libertarian political scientist at the American Enterprise Institute in

Washington, D.C., was quite explicit that only the top few percent of under-graduates were capable of handling the canonical ideas of Western civiliza-tion, and seemed unconcerned about the remainder.[26] Allan Bloom's animus was the curricular decline experienced by undergraduates in the most selec-tive colleges. It is useful, nevertheless, to project those issues upon the plebi-an portions of higher education. What are the purposes of higher education among the other 75%?

Clearly the private economic benefits of higher education loom very large in the minds of many students in community colleges and in non-elite 4-year colleges. Undergraduates who are the first in their families to have at-tended college typically view higher education as a route to upward mobility, a shot at a credential, a stepping-stone to a well-paying job. Merely getting to college represents a major achievement, and working one's way through college is often a struggle. These students have seen at close range what it means to work at minimum-wage jobs or raise a family on a low income, and most are strongly committed to rising above that station. Consequently, while some non-traditional students are nevertheless drawn to liberal arts majors, the majority play it safe and opt for majors with clear career paths.

This situation has provoked decades-long critiques about whether mass higher education is offering an inferior education to disadvantaged students. In some accounts, college is equated to a confidence game in which unwitting students are callously misled with regard to their chances of graduation. The temperature of this debate is hottest concerning 2-year community colleges. According to critics, working-class students' dreams are being "diverted" by these institutions and their aspirations are "cooled out." These indictments have had an impact. Quite large proportions of community college students nowadays enroll in general education courses with an eye to transferring to BA majors in 4-year colleges, rather than opting for the most applied 2-year courses of study.

Whether following the dream of a 4-year degree is a good or a bad strat-egy for upward mobility remains a matter of dispute. We know that graduates of certain applied 2-year AA degrees—especially those in medical and techni-cal fields—on average earn more than graduates of many BA majors. So the less prestigious vocational track may be the safest bet in purely economic terms. We also know that degree completion rates at less selective colleges are low: the majority of students do not complete a degree, whether at the associate's or bachelor's level. Why this happens—and in particular, how this relates to curriculum and pedagogy—are important but unresolved questions.

Less selective 4-year colleges frequently model themselves on the cur-ricular pattern of more elite colleges, with roughly 2 years' worth of gen-eral education or breadth requirements, followed by a plethora of majors with required courses. The general education requirements typically are not vocationally specific; on the contrary, students in unselective public colleges are often expected to take mathematics, science, and humanities "breadth" or general education requirements in the same fashion as their counterparts in selective institutions.

However, this set of academic expectations collides with the limited academic skills that many lower-income students bring from high school. One adaptation that is widespread at public non-selective colleges is to test student skills upon entry to college, and to require students who fall below certain cutoffs to take remedial or developmental coursework before proceeding to college-level courses. As a result, remediation has become a major part of many undergraduates' coursework in less selective colleges.

College remediation has sparked great controversy. Given our current focus on the purposes of higher education, however, the significance of remediation is that these courses occupy a substantial portion of the curriculum faced by academically and economically disadvantaged students. From one perspective, they preempt what might otherwise be courses with a different goal, whether civic education, the production of "enlightened consumers," or of scientifically literate citizens—purposes identified by our coauthors in previous chapters.

In our view, the more expansive public purposes of higher education advocated by our colleagues apply equally well to students from less privileged backgrounds as to privileged undergraduates attending elite institutions. Dewey argued that a central purpose of public higher education was to create citizens capable of "deliberative democracy," and by extending expertise to as many people as possible, education would prevent a small elite from dominating public debate on issues of the day. The first president of the City College of New York argued in the 19th century: "The experiment is to be tried, whether the children of the people, the children of the whole people, can be educated; and whether an institution of the highest grade can be successfully controlled by the popular will, not by the privileged few."

Is it reasonable, given their strong career orientation, to expect today's undergraduates in mass higher education institutions to be interested in a civic education agenda? Are they as capable of such endeavors, given the academic weaknesses that many of them bring from high school? In our view, the answer to both questions is an emphatic yes. The authors of previous chapters advocated a curriculum that addressed the public controversies of our age as one way of developing civic awareness and involvement among undergraduates. Students from "the other 75%" have an eye on the utility of their diploma, but they also find compelling issues such as global warming and ecological sustainability; evolution, genetics, and medical ethics; the role of the state and markets and taxation in capitalist society; immigration policy; the moral dilemmas of inequality and poverty; recent developments in science and technology; and our nation's involvement in making war and peace, and its place in the international order.

Having a weak grasp for factoring polynomials, solving simultaneous equations, or calculus, or having limited skills in written expression—the skill areas that channel many students into remedial classes—are not insurmountable barriers to thinking critically about contemporary affairs or civic issues. What stands in the way of the broader educational purposes advocated by our colleagues are not students' insufficient intellect or skills or interest, in our view, but rather the degree requirements and discipline-specific coursework that predominate in today's academy, a mass of remedial and required coursework that rarely rises to the challenge of combining relevance and rigor that civic education requires.

The difficulties of rebalancing higher education to better reflect public purposes—developing students' "civic courage," moral judgment, critical thinking, and scientific and global awareness—will be similar in elite and mass institutions. One might further argue that the need for a broader conceptualization of the purposes of education is even greater in less selective colleges. Commuter students typically lack the "extra" curriculum of on-campus sports; and artistic, literary, and cultural experience that students who live on campus experience. Consequently, if commuter students are going to encounter civic education, or become "enlightened consumers" or scientifically literate citizens, this is going to have to come via their classroom hours.

This will require shifts in disciplinary practices, in curricular requirements, and in the attitudes of administrators and academics. The need for change in this direction is at least as pressing in the mass public universities as in the elite private institutions.

NOTES

1. National Center for Education Statistics, *The Condition of Education 2010,* http://nces.ed.gov/programs/coe/. See in particular Indicator 7: http://nces.ed.gov/programs/coe/2010/section1/indicator07.asp

2. National Center for Education Statistics, "Nontraditional Undergraduates: Trends in Enrollment from 1986 to 1992 and Persistence and Attainment Among 1989–90 Beginning Postsecondary Students," http://nces.ed.gov/pubs/97578.pdf. See also National Center for Education Statistics, *Profile of Undergraduates in U.S. Postsecondary Institutions: 1999–2000,* http://nces.ed.gov/pubs2002/2002168.PDF

3. College Board, *Trends in College Pricing 2010,* http://www.collegeboard.com/html/trends

4. These figures come from the authors' analyses of National Postsecondary Student Aid Study (NPSAS) data for 2003–2004.

5. Students who are married, have a child, or are veterans or members of the armed forces are counted as being independent for aid purposes even if they are under 24 years of age. But unless a student under age 24 falls under one of those exemptions, the student is classified as financially dependent upon parents even if the student can provide proof of a separate residence or document complete financial independence.

6. The figure for 2009 comes from the Current Population Survey, http://www.bls.gov/news.release/hsgec.nr0.htm

7. This estimate comes from Timothy Clydesdale, *The First Year Out: Understanding American Teens After High School* (Chicago: University of Chicago Press, 2007).

8. Laura Horn, Emily Forrest Cataldi, and Anna Sikora, *Waiting to Attend College: Undergraduates Who Delay Their Postsecondary Enrollment* (Washington, DC: GPO, 2005).

9. *Trends in College Pricing 2010.*

10. National Center for Education Statistics, *Condition of Education 2010*, Table A39-1.

11. Ibid.,Table 19-1.

12. These data are authors' calculations from the nationally representative Beginning Secondary Study that followed a cohort from 1996 for 6 years. On dropping and stopping out, see also Laura J. Horn, *Stopouts or Stayouts? Undergraduates Who Leave College in Their First Year* (Washington, DC: GPO, 1998).

13. National Center for Education Statistics, *A Descriptive Summary of 1999–2000 Bachelor's Degree Recipients 1 Year Later. With an Analysis of Time to Degree* (Washington DC: GPO, 2003), 24, http://nces.ed.gov/pubs2003/2003165.pdf

14. Susan P. Choy and Ellen M. Bradburn, *Ten Years After College: Comparing the Employment Experiences of 1992–93 Bachelor's Degree Recipients with Academic and Career-Oriented Majors* (Washington, DC: U.S. Department of Education, 2008), 55.

15. The 2007–2008 numbers come from the Integrated Postsecondary Education Data System (IPEDS) and can be found in the *Condition of Education 2010*, http://nces.ed.gov/programs/coe/2010/section5/table-fsu-1.asp

16. Sandra Baum et al., *Education Pays 2010* (New York: College Board, 2010).

17. Jennie C. Bran and Yu Xie, "Who Benefits Most from College? Evidence for Negative Selection in Heterogeneous Economic Returns to Higher Education," *American Sociological Review* 75, no. 2 (April 2010): 275–302; and Paul Attewell and David E. Lavin, *Passing the Torch: Does Higher Education for the Disadvantaged Pay Off Across the Generations?* (New York: Russell Sage, 2007).

18. Baum et al., *Education Pays.*

19. W. J. Hussar and T. Bailey, *Projections of Educational Statistics to 2017* (Washington, DC: GPO, 2008), 9.

20. Attewell and Lavin, *Passing the Torch.*

21. College Board, *Trends in College Pricing 2009.*

22. College Board, *Trends in College Pricing 2010.*

23. Bridgett Terry Long, "The Impact of Federal Tax Credits for Higher Education Expenses" (NBER Working Paper W9553), in *College Choices: The Economics of Which College, When College, and How to Pay for It,* ed. Caroline M. Hoxby (Chicago: University of Chicago Press and the National Bureau of Economic Research, 2004).

24. Advisory Committee on Student Financial Assistance, *The Rising Price of Inequality: How Inadequate Grant Aid Limits College Access and Persistence* (Washington DC: Advisory Committee on Student Financial Assistance, 2010), http://www2.ed.gov/about/bdscomm/list/acsfa/acsfarpijune2010.pdf

25. College Board, *Trends in College Pricing 2010.*

26. Charles Murray, *Real Education: Four Simple Truths for Bringing America's Schools Back to Reality* (New York: Crown Forum, 2008), 67.

CHAPTER 5

Professional Education: Aligning Knowledge, Expertise, and Public Purpose

William M. Sullivan

Higher education shapes the practical imagination. Among the several dimensions of personal identity, it is the practical imagination that proposes what we can make of our lives, and the things we may hope for, individually and together. The scope of the practical imagination either expands or contracts students' capacities to engage with their lives in resourceful, reflective ways. It was Aristotle, one of history's great educators, who said that the institutions of a city needed to be aligned in order to shape its citizens' acquisition of knowledge, skill, and character so that they would care about their community and have the ability to contribute to its welfare. Schools, like his Lyceum, were to be organized to concentrate this formative process. Even in today's colleges, educating the practical imagination toward such ends is an intensely collaborative affair, involving the students themselves, but also the faculty and all university personnel as central actors.

With the great majority of today's students enrolled in professional or pre-professional courses of study, higher education's effects on the practical imagination of this generation of students will be especially concentrated on vocational questions and themes. Professional education presents students with the knowledge, skills, and purpose of the field they seek to learn. It also frames how students relate the demands and possibilities of the profession to their developing sense of self and purpose.

Higher education therefore has the responsibility to see that its vocational programs do justice to the large task of preparing students to shape lives of meaning and purpose. Within a dynamic but unstable world, the academy needs to provide a professional preparation that is broad as well as deep.

Today's educators find themselves working within a complex heritage. Professional education became part of the developing American university in the late 19th century. Before that, most professions recruited and trained their members through apprenticeship. Learning and teaching took place in settings of practice. In this way, professions continued the ways of craft guilds, though the learned professions of the clergy, the bar, and medicine also fostered distinctive features: complex cognitive knowledge, trained capacities of skillful practice, and commitment to the purposes espoused by the professional community. Within the intense, face-to-face setting of apprenticeship, professional training also left strong marks on personal identity. While professional education today takes place in more impersonal and formalized settings, it continues to influence the practical imagination. Today's students in effect apprentice through the professional school. Their first encounter with their professions takes place in the educational setting and it is in that context that they begin to become professionals.

The American professions advanced their legitimacy by negotiating "social contracts" to serve the public. That is, the professions achieved considerable legal autonomy regarding standards of practice, admission, and education in exchange for taking responsibility for providing public values such as civil order and equity, health, education, probity in financial reporting, and so forth. The public and ethical significance of professionalized occupations—their appeal to the American practical imagination—is their promise of providing not only a career and livelihood but a calling to useful work that supports public values. The continuing appeal of professions such as law, medicine, teaching, engineering, the clergy and the rest suggests that they articulate a hunger. They promise access to a sense of calling, a sense that one's work has dignity and rightly confers dignity and recognition because that work supports valuable common purposes, which in turn give point and value to individual effort.[1] Even today, professional values of integrity in work and service can build and sustain highly effective organizations oriented toward competence and public service, as exemplified in the Mayo and Cleveland Clinics in medicine. Both the organization of their work and its effects set such organizations apart from purely market-driven or managerial institutions.[2]

At the same time, the rise of the American professions has not been simply a tale of the power of ideals. As students of the professions have shown, less noble ambition and self-interest played large roles in the rise of the professions conceived as "collective mobility projects." University training was sought not only because it was believed to improve standards of practice but because it boosted any aspiring field's aura of prestige through association with the ideal aims at knowledge and science espoused by the academy.[3] The contexts as well as the content of the work of professions differ widely. As disastrous failures of professional judgment during recent years make clear, service to society according to a profession's best standards can be reliably expected only so long as the practices and institutional settings of work, as well as the aspirations of practitioners, align with the larger goals of aiding clients and benefiting society.

Authentic professional values are still vital, serving for many of the most respected members of their professional communities as sources of moral identity and motivation. But the misalignment between professional ideals and the concrete goals of actual settings of professional work, widespread in many fields today including prominent areas such as health care, business, and financial services, place these purposes under real threat.[4] In order to revitalize a coherent professional identity, while acting responsibly under pressures to the contrary, it is essential to articulate a full, civic meaning of professionalism.

In today's fluid occupational context, professional morale is likely to depend heavily on how strongly professional purposes can be embedded in patterns of work that connect the professions to their purposes within the larger democratic order. A chief task of professional education for the new century will be to find more effective ways of equipping their graduates to take the lead in efforts to realign conditions of professional work so that they advance not only the interests of practitioners but the enduring purposes of the professions as institutions of public purpose.

The entry of the professions into the university changed the patterns of recruitment and assessment of competence in the professions. Academic achievement became a value in its own right, laying the groundwork for what would later be called "meritocracy." Beginning in the new model university law school of the late 19th century, performance in the academic areas of professional preparation rose in stature, even overshadowing experience in practice or demonstrated competence on the job.[5] Basing professional training in the university context thereby conferred great prestige on academic as opposed to practitioner values. From the perspective of students entering the professions, the effect was to pull the cognitive, academic aspects of professional preparation apart from its practical and especially its normative dimensions.

Outside the health fields, education became more separated from experiences of practice. Teaching and learning were conceived and increasingly organized as ways of transmitting cognitive knowledge: concepts and analytical tools. These tendencies were greatly augmented by the large-scale expansion of American higher education after World War II. Buoyed by the success of national efforts to mobilize expertise in the service of military victory, the university gained new prominence as an engine of scientific progress. During the years of postwar prosperity, American leaders hoped to extend the use of formal knowledge and analytical procedures to secure global ascendancy in more and more areas.

During that period and beyond, for the past half-century the preparation of professionals has become ever more important in the university. American higher education's shift toward a more consciously vocational emphasis is in fact one of the major stories of the most recent period. Professional work and the "knowledge workers" who perform it have likewise grown in both absolute and relative importance in economy and society. No longer just the traditional fields of law, medicine, ministry, and academe, but a growing number of others such as engineering, architecture, business and public sector management, teaching, and nursing have sought to confirm their professional status by providing university training for ever more of their aspirants.

In recent decades, however, the more intensely competitive, increasingly global economic order has created new and stronger cross-pressures in professional work. The rise of market thinking has also had powerful effects on professional preparation in higher education. The new economic order has squeezed professionals into organizations that are increasingly managed by narrow goals of economic advantage, while more professionals work in settings managed by non-professionals or by members of a different profession. Performance is increasingly measured by impressive returns on the "bottom line." Like the earlier vogue of technocratic management, this recent emphasis on market measures threatens to extinguish traditional values of collegial control, public service, and integrity of craft. The danger is that such a purely "technical" professionalism will colonize professionals' practical imaginations, eclipsing any serious aspirations to serve society.

Developing a civic professionalism in our time will need the professional schools, and therefore the university, as partners. It will also demand further evolution in how professional preparation is carried on in the academy. Today's task is to expand the practical imagination of professionals. Increasing social complexity, often described today as "globalization" or the effects of the "information revolution," has generated great fragility—as the great global recession of the late 2000s made only too clear. The needed response from the academy is to cultivate habits of thinking that can combine analytical sharpness on the conceptual level with action-oriented abilities to understand particular contexts so as to engage with others to solve problems.

This aim points toward a new configuration of professional training that would emphasize dispositions often associated with liberal education, especially the readiness to think of how particular kinds of professional expertise can contribute to larger, public enterprises. The practical imagination of professionals must grow from the craft traditions of the past into forms more adequate to a knowledge-intensive occupational world. But it must also avoid capture by narrow notions of expertise, of a technocratic vision that gives no purchase on a framework of meaning that connects professional practice with the larger task of realizing a more inclusive and cohesive democratic life.

TRAINING PROFESSIONALS AS EXPERTS:
THE INHERITANCE FROM THE POSTWAR UNIVERSITY

The American university achieved its present structure in the 3 decades that followed American victory in World War II. That structure has now become a global inheritance, continuing to shape the aspirations of not only American higher education but of the increasingly worldwide expansion of universities as well. To imagine the future of higher education, therefore, we need to understand it. We have to criticize its misdirection where necessary. But above all we must find ways to appropriate its valuable features while trying to reconstruct these in new ways for very different times.

In the 1960s, Clark Kerr famously dubbed the emerging institutional form the "multiversity." He meant that in addition to undergraduate education, the university now incorporated the additional functions of graduate training and its closely allied enterprise of research.[6] To these, we can surely add the university's involvement in providing knowledge and resources for a variety of social efforts, especially of late the direct commercialization of expert services and products of research. But none of these has been more significant for American society than higher education's growing involvement in the training of professionals in a growing number of fields.

Professional education has grown to become arguably the leading activity of American higher education, in some fields even at the undergraduate level. It shows all the signs of continued growth. For this reason alone, its social and cultural significance deserves to be better understood.[7] In those postwar decades, observers saw all this as pointing toward the emergence, for the first time, of a truly national—as opposed to merely regional—personnel system, spreading a common, upper-middle-class culture of achievement. This culture was believed to emanate from the graduate schools of the arts and sciences that stood at the core of the research university.[8] In fact, it was largely the professional schools that were the strategic transmitters of these values, as well as the knowledge and skills extolled by the advocates of meritocracy. It was, in turn, chiefly through the expanding numbers of professionally trained "knowledge workers"—and the opportunities to enter the middle class that such careers opened up—that the multiversity established its claims for ever-growing public support.

The postwar university was closely tied to the new social and political arrangements that made the national government responsible for the well-being of its citizens in unprecedented ways. That era was marked by vast confidence in the abilities of certified technical expertise to master complexity and uncertainty in human affairs, from technological medicine to economic management to urban planning. We can now see it as the time when technocracy as an ideology of progress reached a zenith. In the professions, the older image of the professional as a public-spirited "social trustee" gave way to a new conception of the professional as disengaged technical expert.[9] These developments had major effects on professional education as well, strengthening the importance of specialized, academic knowledge at the expense of the outlook of practitioners and links to the lay public. Within most professions there was a widespread aspiration to advance competence and social prestige through replacing practices grounded in inherited traditions of craft with the up-to-date discoveries of science. In order to appear "scientific," however, professional education came to rigidly separate "facts" from "values" in many fields, while technical competence was exalted at the expense of the cultivation of moral dispositions.

The optimism fuelling the technocratic impulse was soon overtaken by waves of dissent, much of it based in the university, followed by a general weakening of confidence in the major institutions of American society. By the 1970s, the entire postwar order was in crisis, economically, politically, and culturally. Overall, the era ended not in a triumphant expansion of expert-guided progress, but with the disgrace of an overconfident technocracy implicated in military failure abroad and social breakdown at home. Yet professional education, like the university in which it was increasingly housed, remained a bastion of confidence in the values of detached expertise.

From the economic and political turmoil of the 1970s onward, however, the newly constrained conditions made higher education's environment increasingly unstable. Confidence in technocratic, especially government management was replaced at the level of guiding beliefs by return to an older American faith in individual enterprise and market competition. However, these developments were significantly aided by academic research and thinking in economics and business. The post-1970s creed stressed, as had the earlier technocratic view, the great value of measurement, but it focused on the private sector, promoting quick returns for strategic economic action, as in the infamous stress on quarterly earnings reports in the world of corporate finance. In such a social milieu, higher education came more and more to be seen as a private good that promoted individual mobility rather than a source of general benefit to be supported at public expense. The eventual result was not convergence toward a single model of the "university college," as seemed likely in the 1960s when trend lines pointed toward greater economic equality, but the evolution of an increasingly differentiated system that continues to reflect more than ameliorate social stratification by race and income.

As larger proportions of the population entered higher education, most students were studying vocational subjects in large, comprehensive institutions. Much smaller numbers matriculated at elite research universities or the liberal arts colleges that had reshaped themselves to appeal to an increasingly national and upper-middle-class demographic base. The result is that today, while the inheritance of the postwar university continues, that model confronts much more constrained fiscal conditions than in its postwar heyday.[10] The onset of economic emergency only exacerbated the constraints. It is an open—and important—question whether higher education will be able to respond to new pressures caused by the global economic dislocation in creative rather than merely reactive ways.

THE "PUBLIC USE OF REASON" AND THE MULTIVERSITY

The postwar university rose to social prominence within an environment shaped by the Cold War. Still, it embodied a remarkably optimistic outlook, rooted in the values of the 18th-century Enlightenment. These ideals were perhaps most succinctly enunciated by Immanuel Kant when he defined the practical meaning of Enlightenment as the guidance of social improvement through "the public use of reason." By "the public use of reason," Kant meant criticism and debate on questions of public import by associated citizens, independent of the power of princes and states. The novel idea was that such discussion could help educate citizens as members of a "public," whose activities would significantly influence rulers and governments by generating what came to be known as public opinion.

More than Kant could have imagined, post-World War II Western societies saw the emergence of university-trained intellectual talent into prominent positions in the service of practical and public goals. Moreover, under conditions Daniel Bell famously dubbed "postindustrial society," many of these people were trained in the professional schools as well as in the faculties of arts and sciences. The great hope, which seemed to be embodied in inventions such as the new forms of national economic management of the 1960s, was that university-trained and research-guided professionals could instigate innovations to promote economic "growth" to overcome poverty and social inequality, while also using their expert knowledge to forecast and thereby better control the social effects of change.

While such hopes proved utopian, that technical and heavily instrumental version of the "public use of reason" nonetheless has had major, lasting social effects. The economy, the government, the mass media, and even education became more dependent upon complex and abstract forms of thinking and attendant forms of measurement. These institutions, including corporations, banks, and investment firms, needed specialized expertise to function, opening up more career possibilities for university-trained professionals. These same developments also separated understanding decision making reliant upon the use of expert, technical knowledge from the understanding of any broader public, reinforcing an old American suspicion of "elites" and "experts."

The internal developments of the university, as well as its increasing integration with government and corporate procedures for funding research and accounting for various forms of loans and grants, reinforced these tendencies. As higher education grew from an "elite" institution that enrolled less than 15% of the nation's youth to one that, by the 1970s, was enrolling up to 50%, the educational values it promoted also changed. From preparing an elite for roles of general competence and direction in society, the academy got into the business of preparing larger numbers for more specialized, technical occupations.[11] Under these conditions, the need for ensuring basic vocational competence in the form of reliable credentials moved to center stage. In the face of the racial and cultural conflicts that followed the 1960s, a narrower, technical focus often seemed politically prudent as well.

The long-term tendency was thus toward the multiplication of specialized forms of analytical reasoning embodied in technical disciplines. It was away from a "general education" focused on public questions. In the multiversity era, the claims of the classical heritage to "address the human longing for wholeness and its relation to principles of a just and satisfying political order" were first assailed as elitist and then dismissed.[12] This represented a reversal of the national agenda set by the leaders of higher education after World War II. At that time, many agreed with James Bryant Conant of Harvard that a civilized democracy required a common culture, a broad, "general education," as the Harvard Red Book of 1945 called it. Part of the mission of American universities would be the provision of a common cultural framework even as they expanded their enrollments and diversified their offerings to admit wider segments of the population into higher education.[13] However, the notion that at least at the top, society needed to cultivate in its youth a historically and culturally informed practical imagination was replaced in practice by what proved a naïve confidence in expertly managed technical expertise.

PROFESSIONALS AND DEMOCRACY: AN ALTERNATIVE POSSIBILITY

The problem of expertise in a democracy had been one of the most important and contentious issues in the early 20th-century United States. Before World War II, John Dewey, the most eminent public philosopher in the United States sought to articulate a political and educational vision that could enable democracy to cope with the complexities that had once been the concern of elites alone. This provided a second understanding of a "public use of reason." Dewey urged Americans to deepen their understanding of democracy beyond formal government to see it as a culture and way of life. Dewey believed democracy was the social basis and the moral goal for what he called "social intelligence." Like Kant and the Enlightenment, Dewey, too, sought to foster a culture of reasonable argument, imagining and then testing ideas for social improvement. For Dewey, such a culture had to be founded on a practice of reasoning with a distinctly practical intent.

But unlike the technocratic conception of expertise that came to dominate the postwar era, Dewey argued that while professionals were important to making democracy possible under complex modern conditions–particularly educators, social scientists, and journalists–he also insisted that democracy demanded the general engagement of members of the public. By the term "public" Dewey meant all those who recognize themselves as similarly affected by others' activities, the inevitable spillover from specialized activity in complex societies. This mutual recognition, when acted upon, could turn random individuals into an interacting community of fellow investigators and deliberators concerned with what to do about the situation in which they found themselves caught up.[14] Becoming involved in public deliberation enlarged people's sympathies, Dewey argued, building mutual understanding and developing trust over time. With trust comes an increase in capacities for collective action to solve problems.

Dewey was highlighting a second form of rationality. Dewey understood that the cultivation of "social intelligence" demanded learning to deliberate with others. He thought this was what science, at its best, exemplified. In practice, he argued, citizens had to learn to understand the multiple points of view of all those affected by a problem, seeking to blend perspectives to achieve not just compromise but a more inclusive solution to the common problem. This meant that the democratic version of guiding affairs through the public use of reason would have to rely heavily on achieving an expansion of the practical imagination among the American population. This was to be a primary role of the professions of journalism, education, and social science. For Dewey, the urgent question was how to develop citizens who could think and act together as a public. Implicit in this, but not well developed by Dewey, was how to form professionals who could play the publicly educative and interactive role needed to expand the realm of democratic citizenship within a complex society in which everyone did not think or judge alike. To address this question requires a conception of democratic professionalism to guide an appropriate form of professional preparation.

THE CURRENT PROBLEM: TECHNICAL
PROFESSIONALISM AND THE RESEARCH UNIVERSITY

Professional education, even as it has greatly expanded–to the point where it now dominates most undergraduate education–has also become narrower, more technical, and more specialized in its emphases. While this is a direct institutional legacy from the earlier technocratic ascendancy, there is considerable paradox here. Economic and social volatility has replaced the confidently expanding stability of the postwar decades. Misalignment between stated professional purposes and the actual dynamics of major institutions create uncertainty and weakened morale in the professions–not least, some critics such as Derek Bok charge–in the research university.[15] Such an environment seems to demand a broadening rather than a contracting of awareness, especially among those wielding technical knowledge. What may have been rational in the short run and within specialized sectors is proving quite the opposite for the society as a whole in the long run.

The present, perhaps even more than the 1970s, is a moment of crisis. This time it is not so much arrogant technocracy but the "efficient market hypothesis," the belief in self-governing markets sometimes called neo-liberalism, which has failed catastrophically. Resolution of the economic dislocation is already requiring policy innovation in all sectors, including higher education. But the ability to make sense of what is happening and to take up an effective stance toward these difficulties requires certain intellectual and moral capacities of citizens. Dewey's arguments about what democracy requires seem surprisingly relevant again. All this holds big implications for the way professionals are formed, involving both specialized training and the concerns of general education for citizenship. But acting on them will require a substantial rethinking of the received legacy of professional education.

In university culture, the tradition of "pure research" and norms of analytical distance from the realms of practical life have held pride of place and wielded greatest prestige. The pursuit of specialized research has indeed proven a powerful generator of scientific discovery and innovative technology. In a real sense, the advance of knowledge has been complemented by improvements in technical problem-solving abilities in many professional fields: not only the health care fields, but in engineering, architecture, and the many hybrid fields that unite science with invention. Professional practice today is more effective, safer, and more productive in many fields because it can rely upon modes of analysis, tools of diagnosis, even systems and procedures, such as evidence-based medicine, that bring specialized knowledge and techniques to bear in solving problems. The diffusion and productive employment of these innovations, however, involves more than technical expertise. It depends upon immersion in the complex social realities of particular institutions and culture. It is striking that innovations that significantly change outcomes, such as the model of collaborative health care pioneered at the Mayo and Cleveland Clinics, have come so often from the worlds of practice rather than the academy.

As these examples suggest, the university's typical knowledge regime has proven less fertile as a seedbed of new forms of social understanding or ways to deliberate about common action. Here, theory has often remained too far removed from the complexities of social life. This has encouraged the growth of the view of the professional as a kind of value-neutral "problem solver" in the sense of technical expert. This notion is not purely cognitive. It is sustained by a culture of "meritocracy" in the professional schools, wherein purely academic achievement is not only prized but often monopolizes criteria of merit to the virtual exclusion of practical or normative performance. What is missing in such views, and such practices, is recognition of the necessary interrelation between abstract, analytical knowledge and deft comprehension of the shared orientation and values that make up living cultures. Such understanding comes only through learning practices of engagement with social and cultural contexts in the human world.

Many of today's salient problems, from social marginality and poverty to so-called lifestyle diseases of affluent populations, to economic instability and environmental degradation, yield only to such a stance of reflective engagement. For professionals to deal with problems such as these, they have to amend the distanced stance of the technical expert with the more engaged role of the civic professional.[16] This means entering as a participant and learning from, as well as about, the networks of meaning and connection in which people live. It often means exerting leadership to gather and deploy resources and people to improve situations. This is the stance needed to carry out the professions' public purposes. In Dewey's terms, it is the disposition to join with the public as it attempts to solve its problems rather than to try to replace it.

The postwar multiversity's attraction to the dogma of philosophical positivism, according to which knowledge is restricted to those "facts" substantiated by formal, quantitative measurement, has long placed professional practice and the teaching of practice on the defensive. This positivist dogmatism has also driven concerns for the normative dimensions of professional purpose to the margin of respectability. The value-free conception of formal knowledge, however, has proven less than successful as a guide for shaping professional identity, as has been revealed by years of scandals in the central areas of finance, accounting, and law.

In the final analysis, professional schools must be concerned with forming whole individuals capable of and committed to providing competent performance in the service of the ends the professions are pledged to serve. For this reason, professional schools occupy a particularly strategic position in higher education: they are the chief meeting place of the university's concern with theoretical knowledge, on the one hand, and its educational efforts to contribute to both the improvement and democratization of society. But they cannot fulfill this mission in the 21st century if they do not find ways to reconfigure the way formal knowledge, capacities for practice, and professionalism are understood and taught.

THE NEED FOR "RECONSTRUCTION" IN PROFESSIONAL EDUCATION

The need is to engage in what John Dewey called a "reconstruction" of the aims and means of professional education. As Dewey used the term, "reconstruction" is rooted in his conception of reason as the human species' growing capacity to "inquire," or become reflective, about its own historical development. Dewey argued that the proper role of philosophy was to critically examine inherited institutions and ways of thinking, to engage with "the precious values embedded in social traditions" that become periodically mired in conflict, both with other values and with material conditions that thwart achievement of those values. In such situations, "intelligence . . . must become the purposeful, energetic re-shaper of those phases of nature and social life that obstruct social well-being."[17]

For example, in the 1920s and 1930s Dewey often argued that the economic institutions of unregulated capitalism were such dysfunctional inherited arrangements. As evidenced by the uneven boom of the Roaring Twenties and then the Great Depression, Dewey insisted, economic institutions needed "reconstruction" in order to achieve a social order that would better support individual initiative while providing social security in order to promote the development of the human capacities of all citizens rather than only the fortunate minority of the competitively successful. Yet Dewey was no ideologue. The criterion of value, he believed, could only be developed and made concrete through the process of critical analysis and debate itself. This "reconstruction" was above all stimulated by the ultimately moral question of, "What sorts of individuals are created" by the typical workings of institutional arrangements?[18]

Reconstruction, then, aims to attain better the goals inherent in a practice that has become "problematic," that is, lost, confused, or self-defeating. In the realm of professional education, one could reasonably assert that because the positivist separation of "facts" from "values" legitimates the university's denigration of concern with practice and the normative dimension of professional identity, the widespread acceptance of positivist criteria for "knowledge" in the professional schools has become problematic in Dewey's sense. This criticism is stimulated by the question of the kind of individuals being "formed" by the typical workings of the current arrangements. As we have seen, many critics have voiced concern about the "detached" or purely "technical" dispositions too often associated with today's professional personnel involved in many of the institutional failures of the age, including, as in Dewey's time, severe economic malfunction.

The core of the problem concerns the present dominance of the positivist standards as virtually exclusive determinants of what is accepted as valid knowledge in the academy. This was also Dewey's target in developing an account of "rationality" that, as an alternative to various forms of positivism, skepticism, or calculating interest-maximization, he termed "inquiry." His core idea was that human rationality in its deepest, evolutionary meaning, is a mode of participation in the world rather than a form of detached observation. The usual "epistemological" picture conjured by positivist philosophers and their followers presents our fundamental stance of one of observers of phenomena. Science is said to proceed by measuring our observations of such objects, then testing our conjectures against their actual behavior. That is what knowledge consists in. All else, such as Dewey's "precious values embedded in social traditions" are non-epistemic additions, the result of some non-rational processes of the human psyche and therefore not reliable in the way that "real knowledge" is.

In opposition, Dewey argued that since our fundamental stance is one of interactive engagement with the world, especially with other humans, our minds have evolved as ways of relating to a complex world of which we are inevitably parts. Therefore, meaning, value, and significance cannot be add-ons to some imagined value-neutral impact of external stimuli. Rather, they are the basic stuff of what Dewey called "experience." The refined, detached stance of the scientist, he thought, was a great achievement and its results of great value. But the achievements of scientific knowledge are built upon, and needed finally to be guided by, the more fundamental, social process of engagement, of communication, with both the social and natural worlds.

We always know more in our practices of skillful engagement than can be captured in abstraction. Hence, the need to keep up an ongoing dialogue between our concepts and our embodied practices. The evolving human situation meant, for Dewey, that values cannot ultimately be strained out of knowing, any more than the knowing subject can really be separated from contact with the object of knowledge; indeed, trying to do so in thought has led to unending and hopeless tangles of "epistemology" such as the so-called subject-object problem, the problem of "knowledge of other minds," et cetera.

Instead, Dewey argued that all reasoning is ultimately practical in that the fundamental stance of human beings is one of participation in the world and that it is from the forms of that participation, social as well as biological, that we gain all sense of significance and direction, our basic intuitions of importance, even for the pursuit of disinterested truth through science. The fundamental stance, in other words, is that of an engaged insider rather than an outside spectator. Rationality is in that profound sense ultimately practical or "pragmatic." We are finally concerned not only with what causes things to happen, which is the realm of objective inquiry, but with the point of doing things, with their meaning.

Therefore, all inquiry is akin to translation or interpretation in that it is about how inherited values and aims, including the aims of critical, external investigation, can be better understood, even radically revised in light of continued efforts to "reconstruct" our experience, cognitive as well as social, so as to achieve fuller and richer human lives. Humans are the learning species, Dewey insisted, and modern lives of necessity are more interconnected and deeply dependent upon social cooperation than ever before. Hence, the importance of professional enterprises for social well-being.

DEWEY'S THREE-PHASE RHYTHM OF "INQUIRY" AND PROFESSIONAL EDUCATION

Dewey gave his fuller model of "inquiry" a memorable three-phase description that was meant to describe human rationality in its widest and most dynamic sense. As the example of the professional fields suggests, rationality is a social process of communication in which individuals participate. It is misconceived–though commonly so–as largely a solitary, individual activity. Furthermore, Dewey's notion of inquiry placed the detached, analytical stance of scientific investigation as a "moment" within a larger process of human rationality that is fundamentally practical–"pragmatic" is his word–in that it is a mode of participation in the evolving world. Dewey noted how science has enabled our species to better understand the workings of nature, and in certain areas to control nature in support of human purposes.[19] However, the reason for undertaking the investigation in the first place, as well as its potential meaning, comes only from those shared, historically rooted cultural meanings that Dewey sometimes called experience.

Dewey claimed that inquiry begins in experience that has grown problematic in that habitual activities produce diminished returns on their intended aims. However, he also argued that it was a shared "experience," or cultural ethos, that enables a group of interacting investigators to perceive a situation as "problematic" in the first place and therefore to undertake an inquiry. Purposeful human activity, or *praxis* in the Greek sense, is thus the ground and also the goal of the analytic phase of inquiry. The point of inquiry is to restore, or reconstitute, the flow of meaningful activity, which is the meaning of "reconstruction." Analytic thinking is successful when it contributes to a fuller, more adequate narrative understanding of the salience of events. Human rationality in its full sense is ultimately practical—and therefore social, historical, and narrative—by nature.[20]

The second, analytical phase of inquiry consists in probing the situation grown problematic. It takes place off-line, so to speak, not in active engagement with the environment but in experimental rehearsal. The great revolution in thinking that we call modern science has gradually codified and institutionalized this second, analytical phase of the circuit of practical reason. Approaching nature with objectivity and distance has proved enormously fruitful in the production of accurate information. It has also provided new powers to control and transform natural processes, as the achievements of modern technology demonstrate powerfully. The neat, bounded quality of the observer's stance is one of the charms of scientific theory. Another is the sense of certainty available in theory, so welcome compared to the unsettled uncertainty and anxiety of decision that pervades the realm of practice. However, Dewey warned, the aesthetic appeal of these qualities inherent in theorizing, and the technological powers generated thereby, have seduced some philosophers into imagining that scientific thinking exhausts rationality itself, that information is all of knowledge.

This is a serious mistake. Fixating on the analytical phase of inquiry threatens to short out the vital circuit of rationality. A more expansive sense of practical rationality can help to release this fixation. A grasp of inquiry in its full, practical sense also offers a remedy for the widespread worry that we live today awash in meaningless information, overwhelmed by the production of knowledge that, in the form of weaponry and environmental degradation, threatens human survival itself. As these threats reveal, the great challenge of our era is precisely to reintegrate the analytical phase of investigation and knowledge production with those frameworks of cultural orientation upon which we depend in order to secure human flourishing in the long term.

To see the problem in this way is to grasp the perspective of practical reason. The second, analytical phase of inquiry finds its point as it gives way to a third, integrative phase. Here, the new insights and clarity achieved by analytical reflection gets rewoven into the ongoing texture of shared practices that embody social purposes. What needs more emphasis today, perhaps more than in Dewey's time, is the necessity of regrounding the academy's legitimate concern for fostering theoretical facility among professional students upon the meaningfulness of professional practice as lived experience.

Dewey's insight was that intellectual reflection—the transmuting of meaningful experience into general concepts—is not an end in itself. Such concepts are guides for engaging a richer terrain of experience. The point of inquiry in the service of reconstruction is to unblock the constricted or dissociated patterns of activity. This is at once an intellectual or cognitive activity while it necessarily engages moral and practical reasoning as well. The end is to better fulfill the purposes implicit in a practice.

These considerations suggest a new agenda for professional education. Professional education is concerned with forming the capacities and dispositions that enable people to take up the expertise that defines the specific professions. These capacities must be shaped within highly intricate and distinctive professional communities. In addition, each field has to prepare its future practitioners for careers in a large variety of disparate contexts of work. Nevertheless, in every field the challenge is how to teach the complex ensemble of analytic thinking, skillful practice, and wise judgment upon which that profession rests. The university setting, and even more the prevalence of the academic model of thought and teaching, facilitates the training of analytic habits of mind, the second phase of Dewey's circuit of inquiry. The reigning culture of the research university, including its favored forms of pedagogy, does far less to further the students' progress in developing practical skills and capacity for professional judgment.

Moreover, the relative isolation of academic research and training from public concerns, while it fosters some kinds of intellectual development, has pushed the professions' social contract into the background during the critical years of schooling. It is in this lack of integration among its parts and its several aims that modern professional education confronts its greatest challenge: the formation of contemporary professionals who are both expert and civic, whose orientation is genuinely grounded in their disciplinary specificities while also engaged with the concerns of their publics, those whose lives they affect.

THE ALTERNATIVE MODEL OF
PROFESSIONAL PRACTICE AS PRACTICAL REASON

Professionals must be able to unite theory and practice and not simply "apply" the findings of disciplinary research. They must also relate themselves as participants as well as critical observers of the people and situations they seek to address. The basic challenge of professional education is to provide a foundation upon which future practitioners can develop these complex capacities. This goal is made harder to reach by the tendency of today's professional schools to fragment learning along its three dimensions—cognitive mastery of formal knowledge basic to the field, an introduction to skillful practice, and experience with the identity, judgments, and purposes that define the profession.

During the past decade, the Carnegie Foundation for the Advancement of Teaching has studied the educational practices used to prepare lawyers, engineers, clergy, nurses, and physicians through a program of comparative studies called the Preparation for the Professions Program.[21] These studies conducted extensive inquiry into the curricula, pedagogies, and assessment used to support learning in each profession. This research has given rise to a common framework that provides a taxonomy for understanding and comparing the different approaches to education across these diverse professional fields. This framework also provides a lens for viewing efforts to reconstruct, in the Deweyan sense, professional training in various fields so as to recover the essential emphasis upon integrating the theoretical and cognitive with the practical and moral dimensions of professional practice.

Despite differences, each profession addresses three dimensions of professional training, with different emphases and approaches in each. The three dimensions, designated formative "apprenticeships" to underscore their ability to shape the thinking and dispositions of students who enter the professions, are: (1) intellectual or academic training to learn the academic knowledge base and the capacity to think in ways that are important to the profession; (2) a skill-based apprenticeship of practice: the craft know-how that marks expert practitioners of the domain; and (3) an apprenticeship to the ethical standards, social roles, and responsibilities of the profession, grounded in the profession's fundamental purposes.[22]

This framework categorizes the student's experience of professional education into three forms of professional apprenticeship. These reflect contending emphases within all professional education. They thereby make possible comparison across the different fields. Although professional education in all fields includes some attention to all three apprenticeships—the knowledge base, the complex skills of practice, and professionalism and ethics—each field frames the central features of the apprenticeships differently, and each uses different strategies for accomplishing them. In its comparative studies of education for law, the clergy, engineering, nursing, and medicine, the Carnegie Foundation speaks of three "apprenticeships," invoking the metaphor of the once unitary route into professional life wherein novices learned the practice by literal apprenticeship. Today, these three apprenticeships are usually given unequal weight and frequently kept quite separate from one another. They are taught by different groups of faculty, in different settings, and by different forms of instruction.

American legal education, for example, could be seen as at the academic, or classroom, end of a spectrum of such differing emphases among professions. Law school has emphasized the first, or intellectual, apprenticeship, taught in classrooms through a distinctive style of "Socratic" pedagogy, almost exclusively during the 3 years of graduate legal education. Until recently, few students received direct experience of the apprenticeship of practice, such as clinical-legal courses, while the apprenticeship of identity and purpose might be confined to a course in "professional responsibility." Engineering places its greatest weight on a different version of the cognitive apprenticeship, emphasizing mastery of quantitative technique and applied scientific knowledge. There, efforts at reform have introduced more attention to a preparation for practice that relies heavily on the second apprenticeship. However, even in undergraduate engineering, both programs' courses in engineering ethics and other efforts to connect technical knowledge with social and cultural purposes have remained weak in quality.

The health professions, by contrast, have always emphasized the second apprenticeship of practice, centering most of the preparation of physicians and nurses in directed clinical experience. Both fields also include substantial emphasis upon the first apprenticeship in the form of instruction in the disciplinary knowledge that is important to these professions. In this sense, nursing and medicine occupy positions at the other end of the spectrum from the organization of legal education. Yet in these fields, too, and particularly in medicine, the tendency has been for the prestige of scientific and technological approaches to make careful attention to the apprenticeship of identity and purpose harder to justify and defend in its own terms.

The vicissitudes of seminary education over the past half century illustrate the difficulties of sustaining a form of professional education that's heavily based in the apprenticeship of identity and purpose that draws upon humanistic standards of knowledge and scholarship. The skeptical and critical mind-set fostered by the postwar research university placed the long-term associations between universities and religious seminaries, including university divinity schools, under strain. In an influential characterization of the research university—and the professions—at midcentury, Talcott Parsons defined professions by their exercise of "cognitive rationality" using the analogy of technological development as illustrated in medicine's spectacular advances. At the heart of this great engine of progress stood the modern university's "cognitive complex" of scientific research and development. While he pointed out that scientific knowledge required the complement of a "moral evaluative complex," this lay outside the realm of measurable truth. The clergy and their education, however socially important, remained, like artists and literary intellectuals, outside the inner circle of science-based cognitive rationality.[23]

Seminaries, particularly those of Protestant and Jewish denominations whose members were themselves shaped by the culture of the universities, responded by emphasizing their historical-critical scholarship while giving little formal attention to the inherited traditions of craft and piety that had long shaped clerical identity and purpose. Catholic seminaries eventually moved along the same path. More recent worries about the need for more "practical theology" and active preparation for clerical roles suggest that the transformation of the seminaries had been all too successful in internalizing the values of the academic "cognitive complex."

Overall, then, the dispersal of professional training into three often competing dimensions has not served the larger aims of professional preparation well. While it has enabled the professional schools to make their peace with, and sometimes vault to high-ranking positions within the research university, the enduring split between the "cognitive" and the "moral evaluative" complexes violates the best contemporary understanding of the requirements for efficacious learning. Modern studies of learning stress the need to align teaching approaches with the learning outcomes sought. For professional education, these insights point to the need to reconnect the sundered dimensions of knowledge, skill, and purpose. Since it is the exercise of professional disposition and judgment that integrates the analytic knowledge with practice skills to enact the purposes of the profession, then the key educational point is to align preparation so that students can learn as effectively as possible how to enter such informed and responsible practice.[24]

One way to achieve this is to provide carefully structured opportunities to enact, with gradually increasing fidelity, the integrated performances characteristic of expertise in the field. Clinical training in the health professions is perhaps the clearest and best-organized version of such teaching. However, deliberation about cases and the involvement of simulated practice is now available in all professional fields. These are important bellwethers of efforts to close the gap between informed professional judgment and the too-often fragmented state of professional training. These innovations could be seen as efforts at "reconstruction" in John Dewey's sense of the word. However, the larger need is to move such efforts from the peripheries of the professional schools into their centers. A reconstruction of professional education centered on integration of knowledge, skill, and ethical purpose for the demands of practice as its connecting theme would be an important move in that direction.

If the conventional, too-narrow model of technical professionalism is not a sufficient base, what other resources does professional education have to draw upon? Fortunately, professional education is already rich in teaching practices that foster this goal of teaching toward a broader, more ethically engaged conception of professional work. These pedagogical practices emphasize an alternative model of reasoning-in-action, or practical reasoning. Examples range from more to less distanced from settings of actual practice.

TEACHING PRACTICAL REASONING:
FROM CASE STUDIES TO CLINICAL MEDICINE

The use of case studies in classroom settings provides a readily accessible entry into practical reasoning. Through case studies students learn to enter, analyze, and deliberate about decisions within complex, evolving situations, as in law, business, and teacher education. New technologies now permit a rich repertoire of teaching practices that provide students with simulations of practice. These include coached role-playing and the use of elaborate devices that enable the elements of practice to be taken apart and reassembled. Simulated practice pedagogies are used in nursing and medical schools, engineering, seminaries, and business and law schools. Finally, there are mentored experiences of actual practice with clients or patients. "Clinical" education, or the "practicum" or studio, takes place in situations of practice and directly bridges the gap between "preparing to practice" and engaging in the real responsibilities of professional work.

While distinctive of professional education, these three kinds of teaching practice—case studies, simulations of practice, and clinical training—are not often viewed together, as a set of pedagogical forms that are especially suited for teaching how to reason in practice. And they are almost never seen as resources to be expanded and built upon in a broad effort to reconstruct professional education to address the challenges described above. But they could be understood in this way. Doing so reveals a model of practical reasoning that enables students to enter forms of practice that contain—and often develop—their own distinctive knowledge from the participants' point of view.

This model of clinical thinking as practical reasoning aims to diagnose complex, problematic situations and do so by employing forms of case-based, narrative reasoning that employ analytical theory to solve problems. This kind of case reasoning is used not only in law and medicine, but also in nursing, teaching, the work of clergy, and even the practice of architecture and engineering. Practical reasoning employs whatever theoretical findings or analytical procedures have been found in various professional fields to be useful for determining ways to intervene in the situation, determining the points and place to do so as the situation develops. Here, again, the practitioners proceed through the characteristic back-and-forth between the particulars of a case narrative and the general principles of analytical theory.

Specific professions typically develop their own, often-stylized modes of thinking, marked by their own vocabularies that call attention to specific aspects of the situations in which they practice. These shared understandings enable professions to support communities of expert practice. Novices are brought into these communities of practice through teaching practices that provide students with ways to engage in this same interplay between narrative particularity and analytic generality that marks developed professional practice. Such pedagogy requires clear modeling of the activity, numerous opportunities for novices to practice the same activity, including feedback to guide and improve their performance, so that they gradually acquire greater skill and confidence as practitioners.

Consider, for example, the teaching of clinical medicine. As one astute observer has noted, medicine is far more an intensively "science-using" practice than it is simply a branch of applied science. That is because clinical medicine employs a form of reasoning quite different from the deductive and inductive procedures associated with scientific research. Clinical medicine exemplifies case-based reasoning. Physicians proceed toward diagnosis by forming hypotheses about the possible causes of a particular patient's situation. They then test those possibilities against details revealed by closer examination of the patient's condition as the situation develops. Scientific theory functions as a background context for physicians' reasoning. But the actual mode of thought is a kind of interpretive procedure that moves between general concepts of disease, on the one hand, and the particularities of the case on the other. This process of deliberation continues until the physicians reach a practical conclusion that permits diagnosis and treatment interventions.[25]

In effect, clinical reasoning in medicine seeks to "reconstruct" the physicians' and patients' experience of a situation grown problematic. The physicians' aim is to diagnose the patient's condition in ways that make possible interventions to improve the situation. Scientific concepts of biological functioning play a vital role in this kind of reasoning, as does the skeptical testing of conjecture against evidence, but the practitioner's stance is engaged rather than detached, guided by the therapeutic values of the medical craft. The basic mode of thinking is therefore *narrative*, a story about the patient's situation as it evolves over time. In clinical practice, this takes the form of a stylized re-presentation of events. The *analytical-theoretical* concepts of medical science articulate general principles within a formal system in which connections are made explicit, as in the cause-and-effect sequence in the scientific explanation of events. These principles provide a background that enables the narrator to select which details to make salient in light of what theory suggests are likely to be causal connections. But only the actual development of the case, including the results of interventions, can finally confirm these hypotheses as bases for further action.

At the heart of clinical reasoning as performed by the medical profession, there is a mimetic re-presenting of key features of a case experience that engages the imaginations of the clinicians by placing them vicariously within a context of action. Clinical thinking then employs both narrative and analytical modes of thinking in an ongoing effort to link the unfolding events of the case into a meaningful pattern that can be acting upon—meaningful, that is, within the controlling aims of medical practice; diagnosis for the sake of cure and care of patients. Clinical thinking is thus a form of rationally structured, interpretive practical reasoning rather than a scientific application through deduction. The core of professional education requires first initiating and then sustaining students as they move from the periphery toward the center of the body of practical and conceptual expertise that constitutes the community's most valuable common possession.

EXPANDING PROFESSIONALISM
TOWARD THE CHALLENGE OF REALIGNMENT

The educational need to foreground professional identity and purpose seems evident in the movements to promote "professionalism" in medical and legal training, as well as the increased attention among engineering schools to ethical issues. These directions suggest that there is indeed a widespread problem in the professions, despite the undeniable gains in technical knowledge and problem-solving capacity alluded to above. But increased attention to integrating formal knowledge with practice skills and moral identity focused around a fuller appreciation and development of practical reasoning, while of the highest importance, is not enough to enable future professionals to cope with widespread misalignment in their fields of practice.

As we have seen, these misalignments derive in some cases from the subjection of professional practice to other goals that are inherently antagonistic to professionalism, but misalignment also arises from the very unsettled global economic and social environment in which old institutional rules often cannot be applied and in which dependable new ways of organizing economic and social functions have yet to be developed. Such conditions spawn the kind of opportunism embodied in amoral technical expertise. But they also hold out the complex intellectual and practical challenge of realigning professional training with efforts to reconstruct professional practice and outlook to address public problems.

Under these conditions, professionals must become more aware, and more capable, as citizens. They need to be prepared as potential leaders who can use analytical thinking to illuminate complex problem situations but are also able to work with diverse others, including professionals from other fields and other societies, to effect the ends of their professional purposes in changing contexts. The kind of skill required necessarily must draw on all three apprenticeships, blending elements of analytical thinking, practical understanding, and commitment to long-term and overarching goals to direct the process.

Developing better ways to educate professionals for this kind of civic practice would in fact recover in a new way one of the key aims of earlier forms of liberal education. The insights and modes of thought characteristic of the arts and sciences are essential to broadening the practical imagination of professionals for this task. But taking clinical thinking as analogue, the concepts taught by the university's disciplines, like the scientific background of medical practice, require reconfiguration. Efforts in this direction have been going on in the professional schools for some time. It is no longer rare to include faculty from the arts and science disciplines in professional schools. It is more unusual in today's universities to bring faculty from both professional and arts and sciences units together around such questions, but there are promising examples of such collaboration.[26]

The frontier to be explored is systematic collaboration across the divide between the "theoretical" approaches of the disciplines and the "clinical" stance employed in professional practical reasoning. For professions such as nursing and engineering, as for business and journalism, which offer undergraduate degrees, these collaborative efforts could take place either within professional schools or in arts and sciences colleges. For the graduate professional degrees, the schools themselves are the sites. In both cases, however, the hoped-for results would be courses and experiences that could provide students with a better analytical repertoire for understanding their future roles and the actual contexts of practice, on the one hand, and practice-oriented teaching to enable students to learn to relate these concepts to learning the kinds of practical judgment embodied in skills of leadership and civic participation. Fortunately, the arts and sciences are rich in pedagogies developed to foster these capacities, such as civic and service learning courses, capstone integrative projects, and other examples of integrated learning with a practical intent.

STRATEGIES AND TEACHING
PRACTICES FOR INTEGRATION: A CASE

How might we imagine such integrated approaches taking root in professional schools and programs? How could the apprenticeship of identity and purpose be reconstructed so as to promote a broader and deeper as well as a more competent sense of professionalism? As a final example, consider a course required of seniors in the Stern School of Business at New York University. Entitled Professional Responsibility and Leadership, it is an undergraduate capstone course that completes a sequence of four courses that the Stern School requires of all its students. The sequence is called the Social Impact Core, and focuses on "how business shapes and impacts the world around us," in order to ensure that students "are thoughtful about their ability to influence society as business leaders."[27]

By the time students arrive in the Professional Responsibility and Leadership class, they have studied the four standard business disciplines and information technology applications, as well as economics and other subjects in the university's liberal arts "core," along with electives outside business. Throughout this curriculum there is a strong theme of global awareness and the value of study abroad. Professional Responsibility and Leadership is a true capstone experience. It explicitly draws on both the core business disciplines and the range of arts and science fields while focusing on issues that students will confront as professional businesspeople and, ultimately, as leaders in business and society.

The capstone course, then, aims to help such students develop the conceptual vocabulary for thinking about their careers in relation to the goals and identities they are developing as people. One strategy the course employs to this end is to present, especially through the business cases employed, as much of the full complexity of actual business life as possible. The students are asked to enter imaginatively into a variety of kinds of business life, from large financial organizations to small, entrepreneurial firms, to major corporations, to consulting businesses. The intent is to provide opportunities to enter into such alternative lives so as to recognize the kinds of things valued in each context, while exploring how these fit or challenge the students' own beliefs and purposes. Another strategy is to use the reading of texts, including imaginative literature, as a way to develop insight and gain conceptual resources for dealing with the big ethical challenges of business. The syllabus provides various, sometimes surprising perspectives that students can discuss and employ in making sense of the problems with which the cases confront them class by class.

For example, students encounter cases that generate conflicts between the individual's apparent, immediate advantage and their commitment to an ethic of responsibility either as employees, employers, or as citizens. The reading juxtaposed to these situations is from Cicero, the Roman advocate and statesman, who wrote a short philosophical work for his son entitled *On Duties*. Interestingly, Cicero used cases drawn from the life of his times to lead his son to explore the kinds of moral conflicts to which active involvement in business or politics gives rise. The guiding question Cicero poses is how to reconcile opportunities for one's own advancement or enrichment with a commitment to ethical integrity, equity, and the moral priority of the common good to purely individual benefit. Perhaps not surprisingly, many of the students in Professional Responsibility and Leadership find themselves and their queries, both personal and professional, mirrored in the text. Even when they challenge the text, despite or perhaps because of its distance in time and cultural context, students discover that they can use the text as a resource for imaginatively thinking through the implications of the contemporary challenges presented by the cases at hand.

By providing such classic readings, Social Responsibility and Leadership enables students to go beyond merely stating and arguing about their personal opinions. Instead, they discover that their own questions have a history and can be better understood when placed within the larger series of critical arguments that make up an intellectual tradition, such as moral philosophy in the case of Cicero's *On Duties.* Students discover, if they have not previously, that having access to a past enriches and gives depth and perspective to present circumstances. And, in the Stern School's Social Impact Core, that past is increasingly a global one that draws upon the cultural heritage of several traditions.

But the intellectual resources of the humanities and social sciences employed in the course are not introduced simply for their own sake, as objects of connoisseurship. Instead, they provide scaffolding and context within which the students can better learn the processes of thinking for themselves that the course aims to stimulate. In a word, the course tries to persuade students to take striving for wisdom as a serious goal. The cases and readings, the discussions and the journal entries, are all means toward enabling students to confront with competence and poise the endemic tensions they will have to negotiate as business professionals.

"Professionals" seems to be the operative word in this course. Whereas technicians might construe their function as simply making things go more efficiently, improving the means without caring about the ends, this course emphasizes business as a profession rather than simply a set of morally neutral techniques. Business, in other words, is understood as a potentially humanizing vocation that commits its practitioners, as all professions do, to serve certain ideal values and social benefit. Therefore, the capstone draws on the technical knowledge students have acquired, as well as ideas from beyond the business context, in order to provoke students to reflect on their own struggle for integrity. It holds out challenges and models of ways to balance personal opportunity with societal well-being, technical innovation with ecological stability.

By any standard this course is well conceived and executed. But it stands out for its use of pedagogies and perspectives that are unusual in business programs. They are classic ways of teaching the liberal arts. The strength of the Stern School's integrative approach is that these liberal arts approaches are brought to bear on issues that immediately engage the students: Not only their careers, but also who they wish to become and how they would like to live. This is liberal education, then, but with an edge. As another instructor told us, along with teaching practices and concepts drawn from the arts and science disciplines, the Stern program intensifies and focuses classic liberal arts pedagogies by giving students practice in making judgments that both involve values and require action.

Finally, the object of the reconstruction we need is the practical imagination embodied in professional education. As the majority of students in U.S. higher education matriculate in vocational fields, from business to teaching, engineering to nursing, the professional schools have become critical to the success of the university's educational mission. Professional preparation was once thickly embedded in traditions and communities of craft knowledge. During the last half century, under the influence of the technocratic dream, the academy attempted to subsume practice within more thinly articulated systems of formal knowledge. Neither model is adequate to the needs of a diversifying yet more interconnected society in which a variety of pressures have pushed professional fields, the contexts of professional work, and societal need dangerously out of alignment. The challenge is to bring the cognitive gains of the modern university to the task of preparing a new generation of professionals who are equipped and motivated for the creative work of realignment. Professionals are on the front lines of mediating knowledge and expertise with human need and public values. In order to prepare their students to take part in this demanding future, professional schools need to take seriously their own mission to the future of both the professions and the larger publics they have been established to serve.

NOTES

1. William M. Sullivan, *Work and Integrity: The Crisis and Promise of Professionalism in America*, 2nd ed. (San Francisco, CA: Jossey-Bass, 2005).

2. Eliot Freidson, *Professionalism: The Third Logic* (Chicago: University of Chicago Press, 2001).

3. See Magali Sarfatti Larson, *The Rise of Professionalism: A Sociological Analysis* (Berkeley and Los Angeles: University of California Press, 1977); and Burton Bledstein, *The Culture of Professionalism: The Middle Class and the Development of Higher Education in America* (New York: W.W. Norton, 1976).

4. Howard Gardner, Mihaly Csikszentmihalyi, and William Damon, *Good Work: When Excellence and Ethics Meet* (New York: Basic Books, 2001).

5. Bruce A. Kimball, *The Inception of Modern Professional Education: C. C. Langdell, 1826–1906* (Chapel Hill: University of North Carolina Press, 2009), esp. 166–175 and 340–346.

6. Clark Kerr, *The Uses of the University*, 5th ed. (Cambridge, MA: Harvard University Press, 2001).

7. See, for example, Rakesh Khurana, *From Higher Aims to Hired Hands: The Social Transformation of American Business Schools and the Unfulfilled Promise of Management as a Profession* (Princeton, NJ: Princeton University Press, 2007).

8. This was the view of influential studies of the time. For example, see Christopher Jencks and David Riesman, *The Academic Revolution* (Garden City, NY: Doubleday, 1968).

9. Steven Brint, *In An Age of Experts: The Changing Role of Professionals in Politics and Public Life* (Princeton, NJ: Princeton University Press, 1994), 36–41. See also Sullivan, *Work*, 9–10.

10. As discussed by George Fallis, *Multiversities, Ideas, and Democracy* (Toronto: University of Toronto Press, 2007), 164–177. See also Andrew Delbanco, "The Universities in Trouble," *New York Review of Books* (May 14, 2009), 36–39.

11. Martin Trow, *Problems in the Transition from Elite to Mass Higher Education* (Washington, DC: Carnegie Commission, 1973).

12. Fallis, *Multiversities*, 24.

13. For a sympathetic explication of those values, see Anthony Kronman, *Education's End: Why Our Colleges and Universities Have Given Up on the Meaning of Life* (New Haven, CT: Yale University Press, 2007).

14. Dewey's main discussion of these themes occurs in *The Public and Its Problems* (1927) in Jo Ann Boydson, ed., *John Dewey: The Later Works, 1925–1953* (Carbondale: Southern Illinois University Press, 1981–1990), II: 229ff.

15. Derek Bok, *Universities in the Marketplace: The Commercialization of Higher Education* (Princeton, NJ: Princeton University Press, 2003).

16. For a contemporary attempt to apply this reasoning to the public health problem of obesity, see Francis E. Johnston and Ira Harkavy, *The Obesity Culture: Public Health and University-Community Partnerships* (Cambridgeshire, UK: Smith-Gordon, 2008).

17. John Dewey, *Reconstruction in Philosophy,* enlarged ed. (New York: Beacon Press, 1957), 51.

18. Ibid., 186.

19. Dewey, *The Quest for Certainty,* in Jo Ann Boydston, ed., *John Dewey: The Middle Works, 1899–1924* (Carbondale: Southern Illinois University Press).

20. Dewey, *Logic: The Theory of Inquiry* in Jo Ann Boydson, ed., *John Dewey: The Later Works, 1925–1953* (Carbondale: Southern Illinois University Press, 1938), vol. 12.

21. Charles R. Foster, Lisa E. Dahill, Lawrence A. Golemon, and Barbara Wang Tolentino, *Educating Clergy: Teaching Practices and Pastoral Imagination* (San Francisco, CA: Jossey-Bass, 2006); William M. Sullivan, Anne Colby, Judith Welch Wegner, Lloyd Bond, and Lee S. Shulman, *Educating Lawyers: Preparation for the Profession of Law* (San Francisco, CA: Jossey-Bass, 2007); Sheri D. Sheppard, Kelly Macatangay, Anne Colby, and William M. Sullivan, *Educating Engineers: Designing for the Future of the Field* (San Francisco, CA: Jossey-Bass, 2009); Patricia Benner and Molly Sutphen, *Educating Nurses: A Call for Radical Transformation* (San Francisco, CA: Jossey-Bass, 2010); Molly Cooke, David Irby, and Bridget O'Brien, *Educating Physicians: A Call for Reform of Medical School and Residency* (San Francisco, CA: Jossey-Bass, 2010).

22. Sullivan, *Work and Integrity*, 207–210.

23. See William M. Sullivan, "Preface," in Charles R. Foster et al., *Educating Clergy*, 2–5.

24. For discussion of the implications of modern learning research for professional preparation, see Sullivan, *Work and Integrity*, 205–226. These implications are worked out and illustrated in the Carnegie Foundation studies of legal, clergy, engineering, nursing, and medical education: see Sullivan, *Work and Integrity*, 207–210.

25. For a fuller treatment, see Katherine D. Montgomery, *How Doctors Think: Clinical Judgment and the Practice of Medicine* (New York: Oxford University Press, 2007).

26. For a more extended treatment, see William M. Sullivan and Matthew S. Rosin, *A New Agenda for Higher Education: Shaping a Life of the Mind for Practice* (San Francisco, CA: Jossey-Bass, 2008).

27. NYU Stern Undergraduate College "Social Impact Core" description, http://www.stern.nyu.edu/UC/CurrentStudents/SocialImpact/SocialImpactCore/index.htm

CHAPTER 6

Graduate Education: The Nerve Center of Higher Education

Catharine R. Stimpson

A discerning mind seeks knowledge, but the stupid man feeds on folly.

—*The New English Bible*, Proverbs 15:14

In the family of higher education in the United States, graduate education is the least understood sibling. The undergraduate college is the most beloved. The community college is the youngest, but is popular, sought by about half of the people who want some higher education. The large professional schools—law, medicine, and business—are strapping and self-assured. Some of the smaller professional schools—like the performing arts or architecture—radiate glamour. Others—like education, which is huge, and social work, which is much smaller—may feel a bit neglected, but state their mission gladly. But graduate education seems the most difficult to get at, often dismayingly so.

My chapter has two linked purposes. The first is to suggest why graduate education is so insufficiently grasped. The second is to offer materials for a better, clearer understanding of it. Clarity matters, because graduate education is the nerve center of the modern research university, and the modern research university is itself an indispensable institution. While the term "nerve center" has several definitions, I refer to closely associated nerve cells that have a common function. Graduate education brings together the nerve cells of research and teaching in order to create and nurture an "intellectual community." This community shelters many smaller, neighboring sites, each devoted to an area of disciplinary or interdisciplinary inquiry—for example, history or computational biology.

Research "breaks new ground and builds new knowledge."[1] Teaching entails helping others to explore these buildings and grounds. Graduate education asks faculty, staff, and graduate students to do both research *and* teaching, engage in both discovery *and* the sharing of discoveries, to both generate ideas *and* generously, reliably, and effectively disseminate them. Doing so, faculty, staff, and students educate and inspire (and occasionally irritate) each other.

Students who enter graduate education embark upon a sequence of activities. Master's students take courses, perhaps do internships, and write a thesis. Doctoral students also do some course work, take a qualifying or comprehensive examination, and produce an original piece of research—a dissertation. If they are in the sciences, they join one or more labs. If students are successful, they earn a respected and useful credential, a degree, whether a master's or the higher doctorate.[2] They may take that degree to work inside or outside of academia. If inside, they will probably be the newest members of a faculty, eventually replacing the cohorts of their mentors and advisers. No matter what their precise occupation, the degree winners are prepared to become the next generation of the nerve cells of thought, research, discovery, teaching, and art.

My perspective is that of a participant in such a nerve center in the United States. I am an academic who has been a researcher, a teacher, and a graduate dean. I loved my deanships and deeply enjoyed my colleagues and students. I stopped dancing while the music was still playing. In September 2010, I stepped down as graduate dean of arts and science at New York University. I had assumed the job on January 1, 1998. Earlier, in the 1980s and early 1990s, I had been the graduate dean at Rutgers University.

Although NYU was private and Rutgers public, both were multiversities, serving tens of thousands of students and scores of constituencies. Both were aspirational, wanting to change the game rather than sit on the bench. I shared those aspirations, both for the university and for graduate education. As a result, I encouraged reforms. The strategies for achievement of these two universities differed. Rutgers was determined to join a prestigious club, the Association of American Universities, consisting of the leading research universities, and successfully met its metrics for membership. NYU, already in the club, has staked its destiny on globalization, on being "a globally networked university." Despite this strategic difference, both universities were and are still fruitfully ambitious.[3]

In brief, I write not only as an advocate of an evolutionary graduate education, but as an advocate who dares to believe that advocacy and clarity are compatible.

WHY DOES GRADUATE EDUCATION SEEM PUZZLING AND MYSTERIOUS?

Why does that misunderstanding of graduate education, which is central to research universities, persist? This phenomenon has at least four related sources. First, graduate education is devoted to proudly specialized academic pursuits within a university. This has been true since the birth of universities in 12th-century Europe with their "higher faculties" of law, medicine, and theology. Any general anti-intellectualism or suspicion of the systematic pursuit of ideas in our national life will inevitably wash over graduate education. Indeed, on my first day at New York University, a colleague welcomed me with an article from the *New York Times* with the headline, "The Ivory Tower Under Siege."

Second, until the last half of the 20th century, comparatively few people undertook graduate studies, a point to which I will return. As a result, its reputation has been shaped by devoted insiders, who are capable of positive hyperbole; by participant/observers; and by outsiders, who are capable of negative hyperbole. Some of these have sharp tongues and eyes. Their comments can hit a nerve.

Inevitably, the reputation of graduate education came to exist on a spectrum that in its totality offers no clear public identity. At one end is the practitioner's and insider's pronounced love of his or her vocation. A significant contemporary academic calls the doctorate the "monarch of the academic community . . . the very highest accomplishment that can be sought by students . . . the Ph.D. marks its holder as one charged to serve as a steward of the discipline and profession. If this language sounds mildly ecclesiastical, it is no accident."[4]

In the middle is an eyebrow-lifting picture of graduate students and their professors–a representation to which academic novels and academics themselves have contributed–as really smart, but also capable of being nerdy, weedy, tweedy, geeky, frumpy, pompous, self-involved, and, too often, blue-state stalwarts when they are not, in a red shift, actually "pinkos." Then, at the other end of the spectrum is the accusation, which has its validity, that contemporary graduate schools are selfishly producing crops of doctorates who have served the research interests of their professors and who have done the scut work of teaching undergraduates while clinging to the economically marginal status of graduate students. If and when they finally get a degree, they enter a lousy academic job market, especially in the humanities. The cliché image is of a bearded Ph.D. driving a taxi because no other job is available.[5]

The third source of misunderstanding: graduate education suffers from terminological messiness. Most spaciously, it can be a synonym for any post-baccalaureate education, for going for any accredited degree beyond the bachelor's, which marks the completion of undergraduate studies. More narrowly, graduate education can mean post-baccalaureate work toward a research degree, traditionally in arts and science but now in a professional school as well. This definition is the focus of this chapter. Signifying the messiness is the dual use of the title "doctor." When I speak to undergraduates about the possibilities of graduate education, I ask what "doctor" means to them. Invariably, they say a practitioner of medicine or dentistry. Then I tell them about the Ph.D., the doctor of philosophy, a title that many of their teachers and I hold. They are surprised.[6]

The fourth source of misunderstanding is the most important. It lies in the history of American higher education, which has historically been, and has been perceived as, *collegiate*. As such, it is devoted to undergraduate education. That perception, if less powerful, continues. In 1636, the founders of Harvard took as their model the residential colleges of the great British universities of Oxford and Cambridge, not the universities as a whole. The other colonial colleges followed suit. A young man first enrolling in higher education might be training for a career—for example, as a clergyman—but he would follow a general curriculum, which unfolded over 4 years, not an advanced curriculum devoted to one field.

Not until the second half of the 19th century did American higher education supplement *the college*, which led aspirants to a non-specialized bachelor's degree, with *the university*, which led aspirants to the full range of undergraduate, graduate, and professional degrees. Yale University awarded the first doctors of philosophy (Ph.D.) degrees in 1861. New York University awarded the next in 1866. The evolution of graduate education was inseparable from this comparatively belated birth of the American research university.

THE EVOLUTION OF GRADUATE EDUCATION

Two of the foundations of the 19th-century American university were the Morrill Act of 1862, federal legislation which undergirded the great landgrant public universities, and the then irresistibly appealing German university. The latter influentially lauded advanced, specialized learning as important in itself *and* as a crucial key to modernity and progress. Between 1815 and 1918, over 10,000 American visited or attended these German institutions, at least half of them at the new University of Berlin. They returned to become the formidable architects of American higher education: Charles W. Eliot of Harvard; Daniel Coit Gilman of Johns Hopkins (founded as a graduate institution in 1876); Andrew D. White of Cornell; G. Stanley Hall of Clark; Nicholas Murray Butler of Columbia; Benjamin Ide Wheeler of the University of California; M. Carey Thomas of Bryn Mawr, who insisted that a women's college could and should have a graduate as well as an undergraduate school.

As historians and other scholars have shown, before World War II the American research university, like the nation, grew—and so did the graduate education to which it was joined. Where else might graduate students be trained except in a research university that developed post-baccalaureate education? Significantly, professional education was also changing. Training in the traditional professions—law, medicine—was becoming more fully integrated into the academy with its protocols and practices. Training in the newer professions, such as business and social work, also gained academic status. So did the modern version of the ancient profession of teaching.

In 1900, the great entrepreneurs stimulating and guiding that growth set up the Association of American Universities. Representing each institution were presidents *and* graduate deans. The entire research enterprise could seem exciting, innovative, and in the national interest. In 1919, the then graduate dean of Yale, James Rowland Angell, called the fledgling National Research Council an attempt to mobilize scientific resources in a democracy for use in war and peace. The council, he said, is itself "frankly a piece of research, a great experiment, whose outcome we await with undisguised interest. Its purposes are worthy beyond question. If its methods be unsound, better ones must and will be devised. Meantime it invites your sympathetic support and offers you whatever service it can render."[7]

Some powerful figures resisted this evolution. In 1903, William James, one of the most admirable of U.S. intellectuals, pungently mocked the doctoral degree as "an octopus" whose arms were strangling honest academic values and the ability to teach. Moreover, because research universities continued to enroll hundreds of thousands of undergraduates, with their own curricula and sporting activities, universities could still be imagined as *collegiate*. Nevertheless, U.S. universities had reached a point of no return.

As for the faculty, they happily became responsible for conducting fresh research into a growing number of fields rather than for describing a stable, known landscape of learning. They organized themselves into disciplines that codified these fields, academic departments that then administered the disciplines within the academy, and national organizations that supported them all. By 1905, 15 learned societies, such as the Modern Language Association, had come into being. To strengthen research and to educate the next generation of scholar/teachers, professors now taught graduate seminars as well as undergraduate classes. "Their" students were mentees and advisees. In the 1930s, the Graduate Record Examinations (GREs) were established, providing standardized measurements of the potential and promise of their future graduate students in arts and sciences.

Such developments prepared the way for the immense growth in the research university and in graduate education during and after World War II, that cataclysm that radically changed global politics and societies.

WORLD WAR II AND THE UNITED STATES AS "GOLD STANDARD"

The evolutionary leap in graduate education after World War II can be demonstrated in five ways. The first pertains to institutional growth. In 1944, when Butler left the presidency of Columbia, its operating budget was $11 million. Fifty years later, in 1993–94, it was $1.1 billion. The second way concerns the number of institutions that award a doctoral degree. In 1900, there were 25 of them. Now, there are over 400. The third figure deals with the number of doctorates themselves: by 1900, a total of about 3,500 doctorates had been earned. However, by 1960, the number of doctorates awarded each year had risen to over 10,000. Now, it is far more than 40,000, the majority from universities with high research productivity. The fourth figure is about the ratio of Ph.D.s per thousand of BAs granted. In 1900, it was 9.1 to 1,000; in 2000, 36.2 per every 1,000.[8]

The fifth figure has to do with the master's degree. It represents a revolution in graduate education. In 1985, less than 300,000 master's degrees had been earned. Now more than 400,000 are awarded each year. Enabling such quantitative growth has been the growth in the qualitative needs and functions that the master's degree fulfills. The doctorate is still a research degree, which may be used inside or outside of the academy, but the flexible master's provides many opportunities: for self-exploration; for the gratification of an intellectual interest; for preparation for a career outside of academic life; or for testing the ground or preparing the way for a doctorate.

Together, these reasons for seeking a master's are evidence of the common (if perhaps oversimplified) belief that modern society has become "the knowledge society" and/or the "information society." Here knowledge and information are linked to innovation, innovation to economic puissance, whether in agriculture or manufacturing or the provision of services. To get ahead a person needs to prove that she or he can participate in such a society. As a result, the master's degree is becoming as desirable a credential as the bachelor's degree was after World War II.[9]

The growth in institutions, including the proliferation of subjects and areas of study in arts and sciences and the professional schools, inexorably led to an increase in the number of academic degrees that institutions confer. Some are within fields, such as biology, but some combine fields and schools, such as the MD/Ph.D. Counting them takes more digits than counting positions on a football team. Figure 6.1 is a chart of the schools and degrees at New York University, whose 50,000 students are divided almost equally between undergraduate and graduate/professional schools. The chart would be even more complicated if our associated engineering and technology school were considered.

Figure 6.1. Graduate Degrees Offered by NYU

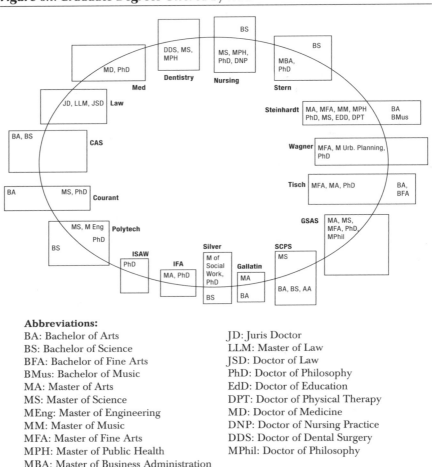

Abbreviations:

BA: Bachelor of Arts
BS: Bachelor of Science
BFA: Bachelor of Fine Arts
BMus: Bachelor of Music
MA: Master of Arts
MS: Master of Science
MEng: Master of Engineering
MM: Master of Music
MFA: Master of Fine Arts
MPH: Master of Public Health
MBA: Master of Business Administration

JD: Juris Doctor
LLM: Master of Law
JSD: Doctor of Law
PhD: Doctor of Philosophy
EdD: Doctor of Education
DPT: Doctor of Physical Therapy
MD: Doctor of Medicine
DNP: Doctor of Nursing Practice
DDS: Doctor of Dental Surgery
MPhil: Doctor of Philosophy

Such a huge expansion was neither whimsical nor accidental. Of course, knowledge begets more knowledge; new questions beget new answers and more questions. More specifically, all of higher education was burgeoning. Fifty percent of its institutions were created after World War II, an extension of the historical U.S. belief that education is a national mandate, ideal, and economic stimulus. The number and variety of institutions is such that in 1973 the Carnegie Foundation for the Advancement of Teaching created an influential classification scheme, which has itself mutated over time. The

Carnegie classifications sort colleges and universities by their capacity for research, their degrees, and now by their civic engagement.

Even more specifically, it is well known that federal policies were crucial in facilitating the growth of higher education. Famously articulated during and after World War II by the scientist and public servant Vannevar Bush (1890–1974), they supported research as a source of military, economic, and political strength. Among Vannevar Bush's most consequential ideas was to fund research in science and technology through the universities that unite research and education. Jonathan R. Cole, in his magisterial history of the American research university, writes, "The implications for the nation's great universities could not have been more profound. His ideas became the basis for an enlightened science policy that dominated our way of thinking about science and technology for the next half-century."[10] Universities, both "first" and "second" tier, would have contracts with the federal government that would support research and infrastructure.

Of course, universities enrolled graduate students, who could participate in such funded projects and go on to become future leaders or, at the least, competent professionals. While they were being trained, indeed as part of their training, they could serve as research assistants, who would work with a faculty member, and teaching assistants, who would participate in the undergraduate classroom. The National Defense Education Act (NDEA) of 1957 unleashed even more money for fellowships and traineeships in a variety of fields.

Some now refer to the 1960s as the "golden age" of the U.S. research university. Time and money were plentiful; facilities were usable—and more. The nation itself was a wealthy superpower. The U.S. university of this putative "golden age" did become the "gold standard" among institutions internationally and, as such, a primary destination point for foreign graduate students. Cole lists some of the criteria of being "the best." International rankings based on research are one. In one 2008 study, U.S. institutions comprised 17 of the "most distinguished" 20; 40 of the top 50; and 54 of the top 100. The garnering of Nobel prizes is another. Since the 1930s, about 60% have gone to Americans. Before the Nazis came to power in January 1933 in Germany, a majority went to the French, German, and British.[11] All other things being equal, surely a bright graduate student would prefer to study with a Nobel Prize winner than with a worthy, but less ennobled, researcher.

More than money, important though it was, transformed the U.S. research university and its graduate schools into a "gold standard." In terms of governance, the U.S.'s decentralizing mix of public and private institutions kept any single, central authority from imposing academic mandates and fiats. The variety of funding sources—public monies, philanthropy, and tuition revenues—achieved the same end. The importance of this diversity in governance and finance cannot be stressed strongly enough. Moreover, the codification of academic freedom legally ensured that a variety of ideas and opinions could be expressed and heard.

Universities also became increasingly diverse demographically. The pool of graduate student talent expanded and deepened. In part, this happened because higher education—both willingly and reluctantly—began its national quest for greater inclusiveness and equity in the curriculum, faculty, student body, and administration. The foundations of affirmative action were dug.[12] The first woman graduate dean at a meeting of the Association of Graduate Schools took a place at the table in 1966; the first American minority dean in 1978.[13] These people were exemplary in their own right, but they also signified the prowess of modern civil rights and women's movements and of the creative, toughly fibered identity politics that accompanied them. Inseparable from the struggle for equity was the exposure of and new prohibitions against sexual harassment of women, an exploitation to which female graduate students had been achingly vulnerable. Undergraduate, graduate, and professional students were vital actors in these movements. A case in point is that one of the most influential books of the women's movement was Kate Millett's *Sexual Politics* (1970), which she first wrote as a doctoral dissertation at Columbia.

In part, diversity was also the result of graduate schools attracting and recruiting international graduate students. Such students have difficulties that domestic students do not, among them cumbersome visa policies, especially after 9/11; lack of access to some desirable government fellowships; and not always justified complaints about their language skills in the undergraduate classroom.[14] It is a blessing to American graduate education that international students continue to enroll. They bring great academic talents, skills, and promise. In the STEM disciplines (science, technology, engineering, and mathematics), they fill programs that would be far emptier if they depended only upon Americans educated (or undereducated) in those disciplines. More crassly speaking, international students bring tuition money, especially to master's programs.

Moreover, in ways that are not always quantifiable, international students, like international faculty, establish a cosmopolitan atmosphere and an enriching variety of perspectives. This helps to prevent the stagnation of intra-institutional academic cloning. Here universities retain their own students, from the baccalaureate to a graduate degree to a faculty job. Interestingly, a finding of a 2007 survey of European universities is similar to what I suspect is true in the United States: "an inverse correlation between endogamy in faculty hiring and research performance: the universities with the highest degree of endogamy had the lowest research results."[15] When international students return to their home countries, they bring the cosmopolitanism and best practices of their American graduate education with them.

Significantly, the faculty and graduate students of U.S. universities fulfilled, and do fulfill, their promise to do great research and to train great researchers. They have been, and are, deep, innovative, and creative. Of the leading new industries in the United States, perhaps 80% are based in discoveries made in these "gold standard" institutions. Jonathan R. Cole lists some of the inventions that originated in research universities: the laser, magnetic resonance imaging, FM radio, the algorithm for Google searches, Global Positioning Systems; DNA fingerprinting; fetal monitoring, scientific cattle breeding, advanced methods of surveying public opinion and, he adds sardonically, "even Viagra."[16]

"GOLD STANDARD," "GOLDEN CALF," OR GILT?

The research university and graduate education in the United States still represent the "gold standard," and rightly so. However, the 1960s were a bloody as well as a triumphant age. It was the decade of wars, assassinations, political and social turmoil (including the civil rights and women's movements), and fierce student protests. They accused the university of being an impersonal bureaucracy that was complicit in racism, the birth of the national security state, and the death of hundreds of thousands, if not millions, in Vietnam and elsewhere. Graduate students were being both seduced and dragooned into this corrupt apparatus. In an example of actions breeding reactions, some protests were over the same policies of federal funding that had made the universities such powerhouses of learning. I remember vivid, explicit posters at Columbia during the protests of 1960s on that campus that named professors on federal grants and blamed them for using their research dollars to support a murderous war in Vietnam. The charges that the research university was putting profits above academic values both echoed older cries by such critics as Thorstein Veblen (1857–1929) and anticipated the accusations, only too common now, that the university is nothing but a business, the "corporate university."

As the 1960s gave way to 1970s, it became apparent that the gold of the "gold standard" lacked the bristling security of Fort Knox. Self-scrutiny, anxiety, and nervousness flowed through the nerve center of higher education. Because this evolution (or devolution) has been widely studied, the briefest of recapitulation can now suffice. In 1968, the draft deferments for graduate students ended. Graduate school was no longer a haven, sought for both idealistic and cynical reasons. As the long war in Vietnam was struggling to its end in 1975, the "Culture Wars" in the United States began. Not yet dust and ashes, they were and are fought over several interlocking issues: the nature of the United States and its role in the world; race and racial discrimination, both domestically and in post-colonial countries; gender and gender discrimination;

sexual norms; and finally, education, especially the humanities. How should they be studied and taught? What should be studied and taught?[17]

The more conservative of the culture warriors accused higher education of caving in to the protestors of the 1960s, so often young faculty and graduate students, and giving them unwarranted power. These shouters and yellers and bra burners were unpatriotic, anti-war, feminists, and multiculturalists, all of them bent on substituting their political beliefs for the abiding values of Western thought and culture. Some of them were also advocates for the intellectual theories of "deconstruction." Nevertheless, the young radicals were now "tenured radicals." As one critic charged, a tad extravagantly, "The truth is that when the children of the sixties received their professorships and deanships they did not abandon the dream of radical cultural transformation; they set out to implement it. Now, instead of disrupting classes, they are teaching them; instead of attempting to destroy our educational institutions physically, they are subverting them from within."[18]

More importantly, and more pervasively, the 1970s was the start of a deeply worrisome financial retrenchment, which led to the quest for more sources of revenue, whether public or private. Among them have been rising undergraduate tuition and fees. The daunting, haunting question is whether the United States, which proclaims to believe in mass higher education, will, as a society, pay for it. The answer that our great public institutions first heard in the 1970s, and which is now far more audible, is "No, not really. Too bad." As a dean said at the 2009 Association of Graduate Schools meeting, "Higher education in California used to be the highway to opportunity. Now it is the toll road."

However, in contrast to much of undergraduate education, graduate education, especially at the more selective schools, will support a large proportion of doctoral students. The Graduate School of Arts and Science at New York University offers them a 4- or 5-year package that consists of a stipend (in the form of a fellowship or research assistantship), health insurance, tuition, and fees. If such doctoral students teach, they receive additional money. This financial aid policy and its equivalents elsewhere have a strategic purpose. They enable graduate schools to compete for the best students and maintain the identity of graduation education as that nerve center of a university where discovery-driven faculty and advanced students teach and learn together.

However, except in the wealthiest institutions, the overall financial pressures helped lead, without any grand and deliberate national policy decision, to changes in the academic labor force. Tenure and tenure-track positions started on their downward slope, the less expensive part-time and contract positions on their upward slope. Shadowing such a development has been the alarming shrinkage of the job market for academic humanists. If undergraduates turned towards a pre-professional curriculum (e.g., in health) and away from an arts and sciences curriculum, especially from the humanities, how many new faculty would a department need to staff its courses? Graduate schools were warned to be careful of an overproduction of doctorates. The weakening of the promise of a good job at the end of graduate school, in addition to the burden of demanding research and teaching assistantships as a form of financial aid was one stimulus to graduate student unions. The first was formed at the University of Wisconsin in 1969.[19]

For many of these NYU years, my office was distracted by labor disputes and by the still continuing efforts of the United Auto Workers to establish the first union for graduate assistants at a private university. For some these efforts were valiant; for others, including me, they misunderstood a student's identity and intruded into university governance. Our struggles about unionization swallowed up great dollops of time and distorted my relationships with students, especially among the union organizers.

During all my NYU years, only two students ever refused to shake my hand. One could not do so at his graduation. His religion forbade him to touch a woman who was not a family member. He carefully explained his situation before the ceremony. We then greeted each other on stage in our caps and gowns with dignity and distance. As for the second student, I approached him outside of a main building. He stuffed his hands behind his back and said, "I will shake your hand when you sign our contract." He then reinforced this message on a defiant blog.

Such rejections could mingle with a residual respect for my office. I saw one student on the street, who had often lectured me about Marx's theory of labor at meetings—as if at best the only Marx I might know was Harpo. She was carrying some picket signs. "Hi," I said cheerfully. She glared at me, and then shouted "Fuck you." But then, as if a repressed sense of hierarchy returned, she added, "Dean Stimpson."

A statistical snapshot of doctoral students today shows the consequences of some of these evolutionary (or devolutionary) steps.[20] Among its features are:

- Graduate education is growing. Since 1958, the average annual growth of doctoral education has been 3.6%. However, much of this has been in science and engineering. Since the mid-1970s, the number of doctorates here has nearly doubled. Other fields seem stuck.
- The growth in science and engineering depends upon temporary visa holders. In 1989, 27% of all science and engineering doctorates went to them; in 2009, that figure was 37%. Enrollment in science and engineering far exceeds that in other fields. From 1999 to 2009, 83% of the doctorates awarded to temporary visa holders were in science and engineering.

- Three countries—China, India, and South Korea—account for nearly half of the doctorates awarded to temporary visa holders. They bring great talents to graduate education. However, these countries are now expanding their own university systems, which will no doubt seek to enroll their own citizens. As national reports have warned, if the "pipeline" bringing in international talent narrows, the current "pipeline" of domestic talent is not wide enough to make up for it.

- Graduate education is more gender balanced. Since 2002, women have earned a majority of all doctorates awarded to U.S. citizens and permanent residents. They earn nearly one-third of the doctorates awarded to temporary visa holders. In 2009, women—including U.S. citizens, permanent residents, and temporary visa holders—earned nearly 47% of all research doctorates. Most of this growth has been in science and engineering, which traditionally was the province of men. In 1989, women earned 29% of all science and engineering doctorates; in 2009, that figure was 42%.

- Racial and ethnic diversity is better, although not reflective of U.S. demography. The number of doctoral degrees awarded to African Americans has doubled since 1989; the number of Hispanic doctorate recipients has tripled. The latter figure is now about 7% of the total. Blacks earn more doctorates in education and other nonscience and engineering fields than any other minority group, but Hispanics are the largest minority group in the social sciences and humanities.

- The families of doctoral recipients are themselves becoming more educated. The proportion of them from families in which neither parent has earned a high school degree is going down. No doubt reflecting American socioeconomic realities, the parents of Asian and White doctoral recipients have more education than the parents of underrepresented minority doctoral recipients.

- New doctorates have taken longer to complete a degree in non-science and engineering fields than in science and engineering. I suggest this is: (1) because graduate students in science and engineering will do their research within the coherent community of a laboratory; (2) because science and engineering may offer more consistent funding in the form of research assistantships; (3) because of national norms and expectations; and (4) because many fields in the humanities and social sciences demand foreign languages, fieldwork, and extensive archival work. Not surprisingly, students in science and engineering and the social sciences incur less debt than in other fields.

THE FORCES OF GLOBALIZATION AND REFORM

My earlier comments about temporary visa holders anticipate the need to think about globalization and graduate education. Graduate education in the United States is reeling and dancing through profound social and cultural upheavals on a global scale. Ignorance of them is not an option. Research, development, and innovation—in both public and private institutions—have brought us the magnificent new technologies of information and communication, some invented by graduate students. I started using e-mail shortly before I came to NYU. I was then such a naïf that I wrote out the symbol "@" as the word "at," and wondered why messages would not go through. The new technologies are transforming the ways in which we acquire, store, and manipulate information; the ways in which we teach locally and globally; and the ways in which we create, organize, and govern our academic communities. What would my networks be like if I were not catharine.stimpson@nyu.edu?[21]

These technologies have so enabled communications, commerce, networks, and travel that "Global Society" has joined "The Knowledge Society" and "The Information Society" as a name for our era. When we look at satellite photographs of planet earth, we see how much we share land, water, and air. Knowledge, information, art, and people flow across national borders. Of course, scholars have always crossed borders and been influential shapers of cosmopolitanism. Among the origins of the AAU was an attempt to manage relations among American and European universities. In January 1900 Charles W. Eliot of Harvard, Seth Low of Columbia, Daniel C. Gilman of Johns Hopkins, William Rainey Harper of Chicago, and Benjamin Ide Wheeler of Berkeley cordially invited select fellow presidents to meet at a conference in Chicago in February 1900. Their agenda was to clarify relations between their students and foreign universities. However, today's borders crossings involve many more people, ideas, and things moving to many more places around the world, and doing so much more rapidly.

Yet the nation-state is still powerful, some increasingly so. The United States may be the Gold Standard of research universities, but other countries are in on the gold rush. Countries such as Australia, Canada, China, Germany, Great Britain, India, and Korea are building and rebuilding their universities. Between 1998 and 2006, the number of doctorates in OECD (Organisation for Economic Co-operation and Development) countries increased by 40%; in Japan by 46%.[22] Authoritarian and democratic societies alike want *their* university. In 2010, Kazakhstan established Nazabayev University, named after its president. It will become, he said at the opening ceremony, "a national brand of Kazakhstan." The country simultaneously planned to stop paying to send many Kazakhstani students abroad.[23] In the face of such nationalism and such attempts to staunch the "brain drain" to more developed universities, no U.S. graduate school can lazily expect automatic supremacy.

The fear that America is becoming but one pole in a multipolar world instead of the biggest, toughest, baddest pole of them all overlaps with and stimulates fear that American educators from pre-K through the post-baccalaureate experience cannot cope with America's diminished role in a changing world. One result is the growth in the number of performance assessments to make sure that we are doing the job that needs to be done in the new world order.[24]

In response, some people do evoke that putative "golden age" of research and graduate education in the 1960s, now vanished, during which public and private funds were plentiful. Others, who comprise a far larger and very different group, reject the politics of nostalgia. Instead, they put pressure on all of higher education by offering a stark choice: change or go into receivership. Re-engineer, re-imagine, re-envision, re-boot, re-set, think outside that box. Use your power and authority to be responsive, to adapt, to improve. That is the marching order. I even published an essay in a *Chronicle of Higher Education* (June 18, 2004) with the title of "Reclaiming the Mission of Graduate Education" that compared higher education to pre-bailout Detroit.

To be sure, graduate education's self-scrutiny began much earlier, in the 1920s with the first assessments done by the president of Ohio University. Then in the 1970s, that decade of pride and anxiety, self-scrutiny became even more imperative. Graduate education was now a big deal. Educators and policy makers had to learn what it was all about. A National Board on Graduate Education, established in 1971 by the Conference Board of the Associated Research Council, issued six reports from 1972 to 1975. Among the question was whether all these new doctoral programs were churning out an excess of doctorates. Was supply outstripping demand?

Encouragingly, the history of higher education in the United States is a history of re-engineering, and so on and so forth, that self-scrutiny and necessity breed. In the 17th century, those colonial founders of Harvard College were re-setting Cambridge University in the sacred laboratory of the city on a hill in the wilderness. In the 19th-century, intrepid pioneers were re-setting the American College for the women and the African Americans whom that college was rejecting as students. In that same century, the creators of the American research university were re-setting the German research university, which itself bristled with innovation, for the industrializing United States. After World War II, the community colleges, with some thin roots in the early 20th century, flourished.

The most intensely self-conscious re-engineering of graduate education began in the 1990s within a wide variety of places: individual graduate schools, national organizations, federal agencies, and foundations. For example, both the Council of Graduate Schools, a national organization, and the Andrew W. Mellon Foundation, another national organization, have been and are concerned about "time-to-degree," how long the path between enrollment and graduation should stretch.[25] For graduate school leads to a career or to the next phase of a life, it is neither a career nor a permanent life.

The names of some of these efforts signify the reforming spirit. Preparing Future Faculty (PFF), which started in 1993 as a collaboration between the Council of Graduate Schools (CGS) and the Association of American Colleges and Universities (AAC&U), sought to give doctoral students a far richer menu of teaching experiences than they had been receiving. "Re-envisioning the Ph.D.," in a concluding conference in 2000, submitted seven recommendations for immediate action. Among them were more collaborations for change; more attention to preparation for teaching; a more spacious vision of the roles within and outside of the academy that doctorates could assume; more transparency about what graduate education entails; and the creation of a clearinghouse of best practices and innovative ideas. The Integrative Graduate Education and Research Traineeship Program (IGERT), which the National Science Foundation initiated in 1997, is to support graduate students who can be more collaborative, interdisciplinary, flexible, and diverse leaders. Then, from 2000–2005, the Woodrow Wilson National Fellowship Foundation organized the "Responsive Ph.D.," which worked with 20 universities to implement the four "Ps": new paradigms, new practices, new people, new partnerships.

Sorting through the literature of re-engineering, re-setting, re-booting, re-seeding, and experimentation, one can perceive four categories of activity. Collectively, they document the good, the bad, and the ugly about graduation education. Because graduate education is an academic activity, the first category is the most fundamental to me. It contains *what graduate schools teach*, our ideas, the curriculum of disciplinary and interdisciplinary programs, the academic and intellectual substance of our offerings, and the methods we use to evaluate how good graduate education is academically.[26] How competent, deep, questioning, and inspiring is the journey of inquiry and discovery, with all its trials and errors?

Two open questions are of particular importance as both knowledge and our assessment of what crucial knowledge might be are changing rapidly. First, is graduate education capable of teaching both depth—mining and minding a specialty—and breadth—the ability to understand other specialties and do crossover work with them? Second, since the rise of the research university, graduate education has been responsible for the definition, well-being, and refreshment of the academic disciplines. Is it going to have the resources and wit to preserve older but essential fields, such as the European

languages, and still support newly appealing but equally essential fields, such
as Arabic and Chinese?

The second of the four categories is the description and measurement *of
our structure and performance within that structure*, those studies and assessments
that have grown increasingly complex and quantitative since the first one in
the 1920s. Unfortunately, despite their sophistication, these studies rarely
capture the feel of graduate programs and the feelings within them. The psy-
chological is left to individual witnesses, the humanists, and academic novels.
Fortunately, these studies do tell us a lot about programs nationally and internationally and about students within U.S. programs: their slowly increasing diversity; their internationalism; the trajectory of their graduate student
careers, with the ghastly rates of attrition and lengthy times to the completion
of a degree; and the disturbing conclusions from a major research study at
the University of California that our graduate students are *less* likely to want
a research career after being in a doctoral program that is not family friendly.
Much less adequately documented is placement, what students do with their
degrees.[27]

The third category comprises the extensive prescriptions and remedies
for the illnesses of graduate education that studies have diagnosed, in brief,
what should be done. Precisely how can graduate education and the protocols
of graduate programs become more transparent? How can programs shorten
time to degree and increase completion rates? How can a school offer more
master's and interdisciplinary programs? How can overly large doctoral programs be trimmed? How can teaching be taught? How can graduate education become more diverse? How can graduate students be happier, more
entrepreneurial, of greater public service? And how can graduate schools
enter into sustaining partnerships among the disciplines, with other U.S. and
international academic institutions, with business, and with the public? Answers to these questions are in the literature and on the websites.

The fourth category, in which the Council of Graduate Schools (CGS)
has been a leader, is to make the case for graduate education, *why it matters,*
especially if graduate schools and deans do their job and shape up. Seeking to influence public perceptions, policy, and the allocation of resources,
advocacy statements stress the links among graduate education, innovation,
economic strength, and national competitiveness. For example, a 2008 CGS
pamphlet writes strongly about the inseparability of "U.S. graduate education, the production of knowledge, and economic and social prosperity."
Then, drawing on the Jeffersonian tradition, it goes on to promise that graduate schools produce more than knowledge. They engender an educated citizenry "that can promote and defend our democratic ideals."[28]

However, this pamphlet entangles graduate education in a familiar contradiction: it calls upon it *both* to increase national competitiveness *and* to

form global partnerships. How can U.S. graduate education *both* serve a competitive nation *and* serve a world in which the United States may not be the nerve center that controls all other nerve centers? Those founders of Association of American Universities (AAU), in debt to the 19th-century German university, were posing their Euro-American version of this question.

The contradiction dissolves if one realizes that one can serve the United States by doing the strongest possible research and teaching, by being the Gold Standard of universities. Maintaining such a position demands entering into partnerships internally and externally. No institution can go it alone in the global intellectual economy. To shift the metaphor, graduate education, like basketball players who leave their individual teams to join together for an all-star game or Olympic event, can be both competitive and collaborative. Today, intellectually serious graduate education—and no other kind is worth it—can be both independent and interdependent.

My experience as an American graduate dean taught me this truth. I tried my darnedest to help improve a U.S. university. That was my vocation. Simultaneously, I was happily a party to the negotiation of a series of global agreements that promised intellectual exchanges and the possibility of joint degrees between institutions. I was not an anomaly among graduate deans. For example, it was obvious that New York University should work with a major graduate program in economics in China. Such agreements are way stations to global universities that might be able to swap academic credits among nations as easily as they are now transferred among institutions in the United States.

Yet the whiff of a ghost as well as a contradiction haunts the useful, admirable materials about reforms in graduate education. From time to time, the ghost materializes and then it dematerializes again. It is the question of the current tenured faculty: the fully employed graduate mentors, advisers, investigators, sages, and savants. To be sure, the wrenching issue of the current academic labor market, especially in the humanities, is very much in the foreground of our individual and collective consciousness. That market is losing the tenured jobs that many doctoral students could fill. Will the current tenured faculty evolve and become more aggressive, imaginative collaborators for change? Some are; some will be. But will their numbers increase?

The resistance to change has various sources. One is a hang-over of the 1960s, that suspicion of authority, that attitude of "us" against "them," now most forcefully seen in lacerations of the "corporate university" in which administrators putatively revel in the toxic tangos of bean counting. Another source, which crosses generations, consists of faculty in research intensive universities who want to focus on doctoral education and dismiss master's education as the province of the insufficiently lettered and the insufficiently skilled.

When I had my 5-year review as graduate dean, the visiting reviewers said that I had to do more explaining of one of my initiatives, the establishment of a "master's college" that would serve our thousands of tuition-paying master's students. The faculty, I was told, didn't know why I was investing my time and energy into master's education. To my relief, resistance ebbed, and the master's college started up in 2007. Quite possibly, an unconscious motive for the desire to focus on doctoral education is the hope for descendants, for a legacy, for a cadre of "my" doctoral students who will extend my family of ideas. If one has lived for one's ideas, research, and scholarship, the possibility that they might not live beyond one is existentially as painful as the fear of death itself. Such are the tender human realities within the nerve center of graduate education.

In the cold light of an America in recession and partial recovery, I see an academic labor market in which tenured jobs will not grow, although full-time contract positions may do so. Graduate deans, responsible for educating the next generation of researchers and scholars and teachers, can reduce the supply of doctorates trained to seek only tenured jobs. That will help. Universities and professional associations can work for good conditions for contract teachers. That, too, will help.

The most difficult political act is neither of the above, but to end the law that forbids the setting of any fixed age for academic retirement. England has such an age. The United States does not. If the United States did, I admit, I might have been forced into retirement a few years ago. The cossets and privileges of a tenured slot in a college or university are, of course, another source of resistance to change. Why rearrange the furniture if the chair is comfy? If graduate students are to regenerate our faculties (all puns intended), if graduate students are eventually to make faculties even greater springs of innovative research and teaching, we cannot sustain both tenure and a tenured job that a faculty member can hold as long as he or she wants. To permit both conditions to continue is to put a chokehold on the future. Between working for tenure, with its connections to the large social value of academic freedom, and working for a legally enforceable retirement age, with its connections to individual happiness, how can I choose anything but working for tenure?

Yet even in the coldest and most unsparing of recessionary lights, my hopes for graduate education flare more brightly than they flicker. Their fuel is the sheer quality of the work that faculty and graduate students are generating together. To be sure, more and more wonderful inventions, discoveries, and ideas will emanate from research institutions outside of the United States. But, to speak New Yorkese, the United States is not yet chopped liver. Moreover, at their strongest, our advanced communities of inquiry are morally charged. They can embody what I call *humane excellence*. Our morality, when in action, is a global magnet even in the most competitive of conditions.

The trinity of values embedded in humane excellence in graduate education consists first of integrity, the absolute insistence that the work in our graduate schools must be trustworthy and honestly done. If mistakes happen, and they will, they will be corrected. The second value is the belief in mutual respect among all learners, the repudiation of bullying and harassment and diminution of others. Such is the ethics of a decent cosmopolitanism. The third value, which bonds and binds to the other two, is the hard-won ability to practice academic freedom. Academic freedom can enable snarkiness, hostility, curse words, rancid skepticism of authority, and babyish irony. I would rather hear them all than to whisper, or be censored, or have the voice box and larynx of thought ripped from my throat.

A CONCLUSION (ON A PERSONAL NOTE)

For some months, as I was preparing to leave my NYU graduate deanship, the phrase "I, graduate dean," clung to and bothered me. From what nether region of the mind did it emerge? I cringed when I thought it might be an allusion to a marriage ceremony. "I, graduate dean, have taken thee graduate school to be my wedded something or other?" I suppose I would rather be the bride of a graduate school than of Frankenstein, but I would want the impious comic Mel Brooks at the ceremony. Then, to my relief, the reference became clear. I, a humanist, was recalling a historical novel, *I, Claudius*, by Robert Graves.[29] Superficially, the allusion is weird. I am no Claudius, the crippled and stuttering son of an imperial family in ancient Rome, a man clever enough to survive by permitting others to construe him as an idiot. Nor has Sir Derek Jacobi, the brilliant British actor who played Claudius in the epic BBC version of the novel, ever sought to take my life's script as his next role.

Yet despite all this, *I, Claudius* is a suggestive parable for anyone who cares about graduate education. For Claudius is a discerning mind, a scholar, a historian who writes his own books. Refusing to be the front man for a ghost writer, he has academic integrity. He seeks knowledge. In the midst of a riot that will improbably elevate him to the position of emperor, he hides in a little reading room with portrait busts of historians. He reflects, "Their impassive features seemed to say: 'A true historian will always rise superior to the political disturbances of his day.' I determined to comport myself as a true historian."[30]

Claudius has been badly educated. One of his tutors was cruel and stupid. He has had, however, one good teacher, Athenodorus, who was both learned and compassionate. Claudius's experience has also taught him to respect not only the wisdom of formally recognized scholars, but the wisdom of formally unrecognized scholars. He says of his boyhood, "I also spent much of my time with my mother's women, listening to their talk as they sat spinning or carding or weaving. Many of them . . . were women of liberal education and, I confess, I found more pleasure in their society than in that of almost any society of men in which I have since been placed: they were broadminded, shrewd, modest, and kindly."[31]

Claudius' Rome is a dreadful and folly-infused place. After a bout of civil wars, the republic has become an empire, led by Octavian Augustus. The ancient ideals of justice, liberty, and virtue have vanished. Universities and professors exist, but seem peripheral to a court rife with intrigue and assassination and an overwhelming materialism. Claudius speaks of a money madness that had "choked Rome ever since she destroyed her chief trade rival and made herself mistress of all the riches of the Mediterranean. With riches came sloth, greed, cruelty, dishonesty, cowardice . . . ."[32]

I, Catharine, graduate dean emerita, am not making my America the mirror image of imperial Rome. Such academic disrespectability would violate the first of my trinity of values: to be intellectually trustworthy. Yet, in this world, with its lost empires and would-be empires and riches and poverties, I ponder the possibility of a Claudius as an avatar of graduate education. He may be misunderstood, but he has vital virtues. He can improvise, but he also studies carefully. He is the scholar whose mind is avid, curious, and rational. He is smart enough to attend to the wisdom of the less powerful, and in collaboration with his mind is a defiantly kind, generous, courageous nervous system and heart.

NOTES

1. George E. Walker, Chris M. Golde, Laura Jones, Andrea Conklin Bueschel, and Pat Hutchings, *The Formation of Scholars: Rethinking Doctoral Education for the Twenty-First Century* (San Francisco: Jossey-Bass, 2008), 11. This book is a summary of the important Carnegie Initiative on the Doctorate, which the Carnegie Foundation for the Advancement of Teaching sponsored and which Walker directed.

2. The hierarchy of academic degrees—bachelor's to master's to doctorate—is reflected in the academic regalia worn at graduations and other ceremonies. The higher the degree, the longer the hood and the more ornate the silks and furs that signify rank. This is a living legacy of the medieval university.

3. My previous writing about graduate education includes:

Catharine R. Stimpson, "A Dean's Skepticism About a Graduate-Student Union," *Chronicle of Higher Education* (May 5, 2000).

Catharine R. Stimpson, "Myths of Transformation: Realities of Change." *PMLA* 115 (October 2000): 1142–1153.

Catharine R. Stimpson, "General Education for Graduate Education," *Chronicle of Higher Education* (November 1, 2002).

Catharine R. Stimpson, "General Education for Graduate Education: A Theory Waiting for Practitioners," *Peer Review* 6 (Spring 2004): 13–15.

Catharine R. Stimpson, "Reclaiming the Mission of Graduate Education," *Chronicle of Higher Education* (June 18, 2004).

Catharine R. Stimpson, "Words and Responsibilities: Graduate Education and the Humanities," in *Envisioning the Future of Doctoral Education: Preparing Stewards of the Discipline—Carnegie Essays on the Doctorate*, ed. Chris M. Golde and George E. Walker (San Francisco: Jossey-Bass, 2006), 390–416.

Catharine R. Stimpson, "Anxieties and Trusts: The United States views Bologna and Its Future," in *Beyond 2010: Priorities and Challenges for Higher Education in the Next Decade*, ed. Maria Kelo (Bonn, Germany: LemmensMedien GmbH, 2008), 151–155.

The nucleus of this chapter is my address, "I, Graduate Dean," given at the annual meeting of the Association of Graduate Schools, University of Texas at Austin, September 2010. I am grateful to Dean Victoria Rodriguez for her invitation to speak.

4. Lee S. Shulman, foreword to *The Formation of Scholars: Rethinking Doctoral Education for the Twenty-First Century*, ed. Walker et al., x.

5. One pungent example: "The Disposable Academic: Why doing a PhD is often a waste of time," *The Economist* (December 16, 2010), http://www.economist.com/node/17723223

6. A parallel confusion exists with the title Ed.D., doctor of education, as to whether it is a professional/practice or a research degree.

7. Audrey N. Slate, *AGS: A History* (Austin: University of Texas Printing Department, Association of Graduate Schools in the Association of American Universities, 1994), 47.

8. Walker et al., *The Formation of Scholars*, 20.

9. The certificate, the equivalent of a minor in graduate education, is also increasingly popular.

10. Jonathan R. Cole, *The Great American University: Its Rise to Preeminence, Its Indispensable National Role, Why It Must Be Protected* (New York: Public Affairs, 2009), 87. Other reliable accounts include Roger L. Geiger, *Research and Relevant Knowledge: American Research Universities Since World War II* (Oxford, UK: Oxford University Press, 1993), 411, and Hugh Davis Graham and Nancy Diamond, *American Research University: Elites and Challengers in the Postwar Era* (Baltimore: Johns Hopkins University Press, 1997), 319.

11. Cole, *The Great American University*, 3–4.

12. A comprehensive account of the search for equity in higher education is found in William G. Bowen, Martin A. Kurzweil, and Eugene M. Tobin, *Equity and Excellence in American Higher Education* (Charlottesville, VA: University of Virginia Press, 2005), 453.

13. The Association of Graduate Schools had their first panels on minority issues in 1967 and 1969, described respectively as programs for "disadvantaged students" and "the Black student." See Slate, *AGS: A History*, for more detail.

14. Once, as a dean, I had to deal with an American student complaining about an international teaching assistant's accent. Although the graduate student was of Southeast Asian origin, he had been educated in England, including Oxford, and spoke with an impeccable British accent.

15. Jamil Salmi, *The Challenge of Establishing World-Class Universities* (Washington, DC: The International Bank for Reconstruction and Development/The World Bank, 2009), 21. While 3% of all U.S. undergraduates are international, about 24% of all graduate students are. See Cathy Wendler, Brent Bridgeman, Fred Cline, Catherine Millett, JoAnn Rock, Nathan Bell, and Patricia McAllister, *The Path Forward: The Future of Graduate Education in the United States* (Princeton, NJ: Educational Testing Service, 2010), 20. Nor would the tremendous intellectual growth in U.S. research and innovation have been possible without the great European scholars and scientists who arrived here as exiles escaping Fascist and Nazi Europe in the 1930s.

16. Cole, *The Great American University*, 4.

17. Like others, I have often written on this issue; see, for example, "The Culture Wars Continue," *Daedalus* 131 (Summer 2002): 36–40.

18. Roger Kimball, *Tenured Radicals: How Politics Has Corrupted Our Higher Education* (New York: Harper and Row, 1990), 167–168.

19. At public universities, graduate student unions are now associated inter alia with the American Federation of Teachers; the United Electrical, Radio, and Machine Workers; the American Association of University Professors; the United Auto Workers; and the Communication Workers of America.

20. The figures are taken from pages 2–4 of National Science Foundation, *Doctorate Recipients from U.S. Universities: 2009*, http://www.nsf.gov/statistics/nsf11306/. This periodic report is drawn from "The Survey of Earned Doctorates" and is a major source of data about doctoral education. Six federal agencies sponsor the survey.

21. It is becoming more and more necessary to assess doctoral and professional degrees online.

22. Maresi Nerad and Mimi Heggelund, eds., *Toward a Global PhD? Forces & Forms in Doctoral Education Worldwide* (Seattle: Center for Innovation and Research in Graduate Education and University of Washington Press, 2008), 344, is a valuable account of graduate education globally and country by country internationally.

23. "Nazarbayev University Has Grand Educational Vision for Kazakhstan," *EurasiaNet.org*, August 3, 2010, http://www.eurasianet.org/print/61658/.

24. The most recent is by the National Research Council, which published earlier reports in 1982 and 1995. The current iteration uses only "objective data" to estimate quality. National Research Council, *A Data-Based Assessment of Research-Doctorate Programs in the United States* (Washington, DC: National Academies Press, 2010).

25. Summary provided in Walker et al., *The Formation of Scholars*, 1–30.

26. The Carnegie Foundation for the Advancement of Teaching's Initiative on the Doctorate is the most systematic and far-ranging of these studies.

27. A summary is Mary Ann Mason, Marc Goulden, and Karie Frasch, "Why Graduate Students Reject the Fast Track," *Academe* 95 (January-February 2009): 11–16.

28. Council of Graduate Schools, *Graduate Education and the Public Good* (Washington, DC: Council of Graduate Schools, 2008), 1.

29. Robert Graves. *I, Claudius: From the Autobiography of Tiberius Claudius* (New York: Vintage International Edition, 1989).

30. Ibid., 462.

31. Ibid., 60.

32. Ibid., 8.

About the Contributors

Paul Attewell is a professor of sociology at the Graduate Center of the City University of New York. His research interests focus on issues of education and social inequality. His most recent book (coauthored with David Lavin) is entitled *Passing the Torch: Does Higher Education for the Disadvantaged Pay Off Across the Generations?* He has also published about the effects of remedial coursework on college students and on the impact of requiring a more demanding high school curriculum upon college success. His current research examines the causes behind high dropout rates among college students.

Elaine Tuttle Hansen served as president of Bates College from 2002 until 2011, and is now executive director of the Center for Talented Youth at Johns Hopkins University. Previously she was professor of English and provost at Haverford College and authored three books: *The Solomon Complex: Reading Wisdom in Old English Poetry, Chaucer and the Fictions of Gender,* and *Mother Without Child: Contemporary Women Writers and the Crisis of Motherhood.*

Ellen Condliffe Lagemann is the Levy Institute Research Professor at Bard College, a Senior Scholar at the Levy Economics Institute, and a senior fellow at the Bard Prison Initiative. She has served as the Charles Warren Professor of the History of American Education at Harvard University and as dean of the Graduate School of Education there, as well as president of the Spencer Foundation. She is the author of many books and articles, including *An Elusive Science: The Troubling History of Education Research* (2000), and chaired the National Research Council committee that produced *Preparing Teachers: Building Evidence for Sound Policy* (2010).

David E. Lavin is professor of sociology at the Graduate Center of the City University of New York and also at Lehman College. He is author and coauthor of several books, including *Passing the Torch: Does Higher Education for the Disadvantaged Pay Off Across the Generations* (with Paul Attewell), *Changing the Odds: Open Admissions and the Life Chances of the Disadvantaged* (coauthor), and *Right Versus Privilege: The Open Admissions Experiment at the City University of New York* (coauthor).

Harry Lewis is Gordon McKay Professor of Computer Science in the School of Engineering and Applied Sciences of Harvard University and is a faculty associate of Harvard's Berkman Center for Internet and Society. He has served as dean of Harvard College and is the author of *Excellence Without a Soul: Does Liberal Education Have a Future* (2007) and coauthor of *Blown to Bits: Your Life, Liberty, and Happiness After the Digital Explosion* (2008).

Catharine R. Stimpson is university professor and dean emerita of the Graduate School of Arts and Science at New York University. She is past president of the Modern Language Association and of the Association of Graduate Schools. She has written widely on literature, women and gender, and education. Her books include *Where the Meanings Are* and *Class Notes,* and she was the founding editor of *Signs: Journal of Women in Culture and Society.*

William M. Sullivan is senior scholar at the Carnegie Foundation for the Advancement of Teaching, where he has directed studies of professional education in law, engineering, preparation of the clergy, nurses, and doctors as well as research on liberal education for undergraduate business students. He has authored or coauthored a number of books in these areas, including *Work and Integrity: The Crisis and Promise of Professionalism in America,* 2nd edition, 2005.

Douglas Taylor is professor and chair of biology in the College of Arts and Sciences at the University of Virginia. He is an evolutionary biologist who specializes in how conflict and cooperation arise and are resolved in the natural world. He has published more than 50 scientific papers on these and related topics.

Index